The Children (Scotland) Act 1995

in the context of

The Human Rights Act 1998

Fergus Smith
B.Sc.(Hons), M.A., C.Q.S.W., D.M.S., Dip M

Professor Tina Lyon
L.L.B, FRSA, Queen Victoria Professor of Law, Solicitor of the Supreme Court
and Director of the Centre for the Study of the Child, the Family and the
Law at the University of Liverpool

CAE Scotland
105 Bishops Park
Mid Calder
West Lothian EH53 0SR

www.caeuk.org

© Fergus Smith 2007

British Library Cataloguing in Publication Data
A catalogue record for this book is available from the
British Library

ISBN 978-1-899986-22-4

Designed and typeset by Andrew Haig & Associates
Printed in the UK by The Lavenham Press

CAE is an independent organisation which publishes
guides to family and criminal law and provides
consultancy, research, training and independent
investigation services to the public, private and voluntary
sectors.

Contents

Regulations are 'subordinate' or 'secondary' legislation and must be followed. 'Guidance' is Government advice which does not have the force of law, but should be complied with unless local circumstances indicate exceptional reasons which justify a variation.

'Public law' refers to the State's provision of services for families and the procedures it employs to protect children when families fail to do so. 'Private law' is concerned with allocation of responsibility/resolution of disputes between parents and/or other individuals.

Where case law is referred to:

EHRR = European Human Rights Reports

Fam. = Official law reports: Family Division High Court
Fam. Law = Family Law
FCR = Family Court Reports
FLR = Family Law Reports

HFEA 1990 = Human Fertilisation and Embryology Act 1990

Other abbreviations used:

ACA 2002 = Adoption and Children Act 2002

CA 1989 = Children Act 1989

FLRA 1987 = Family Law Reform Act 1987

Introduction

- This guide is designed for use by all those in Scotland who work with children and their families.

- It aims to provide easy access to, and reinforce understanding of the main messages of the Children (Scotland) Act 1995 and relevant amendments.

- The guide should be used only to supplement Scottish Executive regulations, guidance and local policies and procedures.

- Appendix 1 provides a summary of relevant Articles and Protocols of the European Convention on Human Rights and appendix 2 is a summary of the Human Rights Act 1998 which brought the provisions of the Convention into Scottish law via s.100 Scotland Act 1998 on 01.07.99.

- The impact of that Convention on the Children (Scotland) Act 1995 is noted at relevant places throughout the text.

NB. The most recent amendments introduced by the Family Law (Scotland) Act 2006 and the Adoption and Children Act (Scotland) Act 2007 have been reflected in this edition.

Definitions & Principles

■ The following section provides, in alphabetical order a list of definitions and principles, understanding of which will support a better understanding of the Children (Scotland) Act 1995.

Child [s.15 (1)]

■ Unless otherwise defined in the text, a 'child' is an individual of less than 18 years of age.

Child's Views [s.6]

■ A person **must**, in reaching any major decision which involves fulfilling a parental responsibility or exercising car and control as defined in s.5(1), or in exercising a parental right or giving consent to medical/surgical/dental treatment or procedure have regard:

- So far as practicable, to any expressed views of the child, taking account of age and maturity
- To the expressed views of any other person with parental responsibilities or rights [s.6(1)]

*NB. A child aged 12 or over is **presumed** to be of sufficient age and maturity to form a view.. S.32 Adoption and Children (Scotland) Act 2007 reinforces this belief by stating that an Adoption Order may not be made on a child aged 12 or over unless s/he consents (or a court is satisfied s/he is incapable of consenting to the Adoption Order).*

Consideration of Child's Views [s.16 (2)]

■ In the circumstances of s.16(4) –summarised immediately below – a children's hearing or sheriff, taking account of the child's age and maturity, must so far as practicable:

- Give her/him an opportunity to indicate whether s/he wishes to express her/his views
- If s/he does so wish, provide the opportunity to express them and
- Have regard to such views as the child may express

*NB. A child of 12 years of age or over must be **presumed** to be of sufficient age and maturity to form a view [s.16(2)]*

■ The circumstances defined by s.16(4) are that:

- The children's hearing is considering whether to make, or is reviewing a supervision requirement; whether to grant a warrant under s.66(1), s.69(4) or (7) or provide under s.66(5) for the continuation of a warrant; is engaged in providing advice under s.60(10) or drawing up a report under s.73(13) **or**
- The sheriff is considering whether to make, vary or discharge a Parental Responsibilities Order, a Child Assessment Order or an Exclusion Order; to vary or discharge a Child Protection Order; to grant a s.67 warrant; in appeal to make such substitution as is mentioned in s.51(5)(c) (iii)
- The sheriff is otherwise disposing of an appeal

against a decision of a children's hearing [s.16(4)]

Family [s.93 (1)]

■ For purposes of providing support services under Part 2 the term 'family' includes any person with parental responsibility and anyone with whom the child has been living.

Local Authority [s.93]

■ A 'local authority' means a council constituted under s.2 Local Government etc (Scotland) Act 1994 i.e. one of the 32 'council areas' each of which has responsibility for delivery of children's services.

Looked After [s.17 (6)]

■ A child who is 'looked after' by a local authority may be:

- Accommodated under s.25 (a purely voluntary arrangement under which the local authority does not gain parental responsibility and for which no notice is required for her/his removal)
- Subject to a supervision requirement to the relevant local authority (whether or not a condition of residence or other conditions are per s.70(3) are attached)
- Subject of a Place of Safety Order, Child Protection Order, Parental Responsibilities Order, a warrant to apprehend or keep in a place of safety under which the local authority has responsibilities in relation to the child

- One for whom the local authority has responsibilities as a result of a court order made elsewhere in the UK and which has effect in Scotland
- A child in respect of whom a Permanence Order has (on a s.80 Adoption and Children (Scotland) Act 2007 application by the local authority, been made and not ceased to exist

Paramountcy of Child's Interests [s.16 (1)]

■ Under Part 2 of the Act, when a children's hearing decides or a court determines any matter with respect to a child, the welfare of that child throughout her/his child hood must be its **paramount** consideration.

NB. The European Court of Human Rights (ECHR) has confirmed this position is consistent with Article 8(2) of the European Convention on Human Rights.

*In Glaser v UK [2001] FLR 153 the European court held that a father's Article 8 right to contact as implied from the words of Article 8(1) may need to be balanced against the **best interests of the child** including the child's Article 8 rights.*

In Yousef v Netherlands [2003] 1 FLR 210, the European Court referred explicitly to the principle of paramountcy and held that the refusal by the Dutch courts of a father's application to have his recognition of the child registered and to increase contact where the child's mother (now deceased)

*had objected to both, was not a violation of the
father's Article 8 rights. The Court stated: 'the court
reiterates that in judicial decisions where the rights
under Article 8 of parents and those of the child are
at stake, **the child's rights must be paramount
consideration**'.*

Positive Advantage Principle [s.16 (3)]

■ A children's hearing or a sheriff may **not** in the
following cases, make a requirement or an order
unless the hearing/sheriff considers to do so would
be better than making no order:

- The hearing is considering whether to make, or
is reviewing a supervision requirement
- The hearing is considering whether to grant a
warrant under s.66(1) or s.69(4) or (7) or to
provide under s.66(5) for the continuation of a
warrant
- The sheriff is considering whether to make, vary
of discharge a Parental Responsibilities Order,
Child Assessment Order or an Exclusion Order;
whether to vary or discharge a Child Protection
Order; whether to grant a.67 warrant; or, on
appeal, whether to make such substitution as
mentioned in s.51(5)

Part 1: Parents, Children & Guardians

Parental Responsibilities and Parental Rights

Parental Responsibilities [s.1]

■ Subject to provisions in s.3(1)(b) and s.3(3), a parent in relation to her/his child, has (only insofar as compliance is practicable and in the child's interests) the responsibility to:

- Safeguard and promote the child's health, development and welfare
- Provide, in a manner appropriate to the stage of development of the child, direction and guidance
- (If the child is not living with the parent) maintain personal relations and direct contact on a regular basis and
- Act as the child's legal representative [s.1(1)]

NB. For the purpose of parental 'guidance' only, a 'child' is defined as an individual of up to 18 years of age, i.e. other parental responsibilities cease when the child attains 16 [s.1 (2)].

■ The child or any person acting on her/his behalf may sue or defend in any proceedings relating to the above parental responsibilities [s.1 (3)].

Parental Rights [s.2]

- Subject to s.3(1)(b) and s.3.(3), a parent in order to enable her/him to fulfil parental responsibilities, has the right to:

  - Have the child living with her/him or otherwise to regulate the child's residence (a)
  - Control, direct or guide in a manner appropriate to the stage of the child's development, her/his upbringing (b)
  - (If the child is not living with her/him), maintain personal relations and direct contact with the chills on a regular basis (c) and
  - Act as the child's legal representative (d) [s.2(1)]

  NB. For the purposes of s.2, 'child' = an individual of under 16 years of age [s.2(7)]

- Subject to s.2(3) below, where 2 or more persons have a parental right as respects a child, each may exercise that right without the consent of the other/others, **unless** any decree or deed conferring the right, or regulating its exercise, otherwise provides [s.2(2)].

- Unless a court order permits it, no person is entitled to remove a child habitually resident in Scotland from, or to retain any such child outside of the UK without the consent of:

  - A person (whether or not a parent of the child) who for the time being has and is exercising a right mentioned in s.2(1) (a) or (c) – except that, where both the child's parents are persons so described, the consent of both is required for removal or retention [s.2(6)]

Allocation in the Case of Married Parents [s.3]

■ If a child's parents were married to each other at any time following her/his conception, they each have parental rights and responsibilities [s.3 (1)].

Allocation in the Case of Unmarried Parents [s.3 as amended by the Family Law (Scotland) Act 2006]

■ A child's **mother** has parental responsibilities and rights in relation to her/him whether or not she is or has been married to the child's father [s.3(1) (a)].

■ Without prejudice to any arrangements which may be made under s.3(5) below and subject to any agreement which may be made under s.4, the child's **father** has such responsibilities and rights in relation to her/him **only** if:

* Married to the mother at the time of the child's conception or subsequently **or**
* If not married at that time or subsequently, is registered as the child's father under specified provisions of the Registration of Births, Deaths and Marriages (Scotland) Act 1965, Births and Deaths Registration Act 1953 or Births and Deaths Registration (Northern Ireland) Order 1976 [s.3(1) (b)(i);(ii)]

■ For the purposes of s.3 (1) (b) above, the father must be regarded as having been married to the mother at any time when he was a party to a purported marriage with her which was voidable or void but believed by them (whether by error of fact or of law) in good faith at that time to be valid [s.3 (2)].

■ An unmarried father may also **acquire** parental rights and responsibilities by virtue of s.4 described below.

Exercise of Parental Rights & Responsibilities [s.3]

■ The fact that a person has parental responsibilities or parental rights in relation to a child does not entitle her/him to act in any way which would be incompatible with any court order relating to the child or the child's property, or with any supervision requirement made under s.70 [s.3(4)].

■ Notwithstanding s.4(1) (acquisition of parental rights and responsibilities by natural father) a person who has parental responsibilities or parental rights in relation to a child must not abdicate those responsibilities or rights to anyone else but may arrange for some or all of them to be fulfilled or exercised on her/his behalf.

■ Any such arrangement may be made with a person who already has parental responsibilities or parental rights in relation to the child concerned [s.3 (5)].

*NB. The making of an arrangement under s.3(5)
above does not affect any liability arising from a
failure to fulfil parental responsibilities; and where
any arrangements so made are such that the child is
a foster child for the purposes of the Foster Children
(Scotland) Act 1984, those arrangements are subject
to the provisions of that Act [s.3(6)].*

Divorce

■ If a married couple separate or divorce, both
continue to have parental responsibility for their
child/ren.

■ Such couples are expected to agree suitable
arrangements and court orders to determine with
whom the child/ren should live, have contact or
other related matters will only be made when
necessary.

Acquisition of Parental Responsibility by Natural Father [s. 4]

■ An unmarried father **may** (assuming the child's
mother has not, on the day of its registration, been
deprived of some or all of her rights in private or
public law proceedings) acquire parental rights and
responsibilities if:

• He and the child's mother make an 'agreement'
providing for him to have the rights and
responsibilities for the child he would have if he
were married to the child's mother [s.4(1);(3)]

■ Such an agreement must be in a form prescribed by the Secretary of State and registered in the Books of Council and Session whilst the mother still has her rights and responsibilities [s.4(2)]

■ A parental responsibilities and rights agreement is irrevocable unless a court deprives the father of some or all of those responsibilities or rights by virtue of an order under s.11 (11) described below [s.4 (4)].

NB. By virtue of the Age of Legal Capacity (Scotland) Act1991, a father aged less than 16 is eligible to make a parental responsibility agreement.

■ An unmarried father may also acquire parental responsibilities and rights if he is appointed in writing as a child's guardian by the mother and she subsequently dies [s.7 (1)]

Effect of Unmarried Father Acquiring Parental Responsibility

■ The essence of parental responsibility is that it is a status not merely a set of rights, duties and powers [Re S (Parental Responsibility) [1995] 2 FLR 648].

■ Nonetheless, the practical advantages of such a status would include a right/ability to:

• Receive educational reports and provide consent to school trips
• Consent to treatment for, and receive medical reports about the child

- Sign official papers e.g. passport application
- Prevent a mother removing child from the UK
- Object to a proposed change of name
- Object to child's accommodation by the local authority and an ability to lawfully remove her/him
- Be regarded as a 'parent' for purposes of adoption proceedings

NB. So as to comply with Article 8(1) of the Convention, best practice is to treat the unmarried father who does not have parental responsibility as possessing full rights in, e.g. in adoption proceedings

Acquisition of Parental Responsibility by Other Individuals [s.11]

■ An individual can also acquire parental responsibility if:

- S/he is awarded it by a court
- Appointed as a child's guardian by a court or
- Appointed in writing, e.g. in a will, by a person who has parental responsibility – see below for more details of appointment of guardians

■ Acquisition and loss of parental responsibility under s.11(1) occurs if the court so orders on the application of a person who:

- 'Claims an interest' (and does not have and has never had parental responsibility or rights for the child)

- Does have parental responsibilities or rights for the child or
- Has had, but no longer has parental responsibilities or rights (unless those were transferred/extinguished by specified court orders)

NB. See court orders section below for further detail and impact of recent amendments.

Care or Control of Child by Person without Parental Responsibilities or Rights [s.5]

■ It is the responsibility of anyone aged 16 or over, who does not have parental responsibilities or rights or does not have the legal responsibility 'to safeguard and promote her/his welfare' but does have care or control of a child aged less than 16, to:

- Do what is reasonable in all the circumstances to safeguard and promote her/his health, development and welfare

NB. In fulfilling the above responsibility, the person even without the right of s.2(1)(d)(to act as the child's legal representative), may consent to any surgical, medical or dental treatment or procedure where the child is unable to give her/his own consent and the person is unaware of any parental objection [s.5(1)]. S.5 (1) does not apply to those who have care or control of a child in a school [s.5 (2)].

■ A person **must**, in reaching any major decision which involves fulfilling a parental responsibility or the responsibility of s.5(1) – above, or in exercising a parental right or giving consent to medical/surgical/dental treatment or procedure have regard:

- So far as practicable, to any expressed views of the child, taking account of age and maturity
- To the expressed views of any other person with parental responsibilities or rights

NB. A child aged 12 or over is **presumed** *to be of sufficient age and maturity to form a view [s.6 (1)].*

Guardianship

Appointment of Guardians [s.7]

- A child's parent may appoint a person to be guardian of the child in the event of the parent's death but such an appointment is of no effect unless:

  - It is in writing and signed by the parent and
  - The parent, at the time of death, was entitled to act as legal representative of the child

- The appointment of a guardian does not affect the responsibilities and rights of the other parent [s.7(1)]

- A guardian may in turn appoint a person to take her/his place in the event of her/his death though the appointment must be in writing and signed [s.7(2)]

- An appointment as a guardian does not take effect until accepted by the appointee [s.7 (3)].

  NB. Any nominated guardian can accept without affecting the nomination of any others [s.7(5)]

- Unless an order under s.11 or s.86 exists to limit them, a person appointed as a child's guardian under s.7 has the responsibilities and rights of a parent under ss. 1 and 2 [s.7 (5)].

- As the appointment of a guardian is a 'major decision that involves exercising a parental right', the views of the child and any other person with

parental responsibilities and rights must be sought
and regard given to them as per s.6 above [s.7 (6)].

Revocation & Other Termination of Appointment [s.8]

- An appointment of a guardian under s.7 revokes any
  earlier appointment made by the same person unless
  it is clear the purpose is to appoint an additional
  guardian [s.8 (1)].

- The revocation of an appointment made under s.7
  will not take effect unless the revocation is in writing
  and signed by the person making it [s.8 (2)].

- An appointment of a guardian under s.7 (other than
  one made in a will or codicil) is revoked if the person
  who made it, intends to revoke it and:

  - Destroys the document by which it was made
  - Has another person destroy the document in
    her/his presence [s.8(3)]

- Once an appointment has taken effect, unless its
  terms provide for earlier termination, it will be
  terminated only by the:

  - Child concerned attaining the age of 18
  - Death of the child or guardian or
  - Termination of the appointment by a s.11 order
    [s.8(5)]

Court Orders

Court Orders Relating to Parental Responsibilities etc [s.11 as amended by Family Law (Scotland) Act 2006]

- In the 'relevant circumstances' in proceedings in which the issues arise, whether or not those proceedings are independent of any other action, the Court of Session or sheriff court may make an order under s.11 in relation to:

  - Parental responsibilities
  - Parental rights
  - Guardianship or
  - (Subject to s.14(1) & (2)), administration of a child's property [s.11(1)]

  NB. The Scottish court has jurisdiction to make an order in relation to parental responsibility when it is exercising jurisdiction over the marriage of both parents of a child who is either habitually resident in Scotland, or if the spouses accept jurisdiction, and it is in the best interests of the child in another member state.

- The court may make:

  - An order depriving a person of some or all of her/his parental responsibilities for a child
  - An order imposing upon a person (who is at least 16 **or** is a parent of the child i.e. may be under 16) parental responsibilities and rights

- A **Residence Order –** regulating the arrangements as to with whom (or if with different persons, for what time each) an under 16 year old is to live
- A **Contact Order** –regulating arrangements for maintaining personal relations and direct contact between an under 16 year old and a person with whom a child is not, or will not be living
- A **Specific Issue Order** regulating any specific question which has arisen/may arise in connection with parental responsibilities or rights, guardianship or administration of a child's property
- An **Interdict** prohibiting the taking of any step specified in it for the fulfilment of parental responsibilities or exercise of parental rights or administration of child's property
- An order appointing a 'judicial factor' to manage a child's property on her/his behalf
- An order appointing or removing a person as the child's guardian [s.11(2)]

Circumstances in Which Orders May Be Made

■ The 'relevant circumstances' referred to above are that an application for an order under s.11.(1) has been made by a person who:

- Does not have and has never had parental responsibilities or rights in relation to the child but who 'claims an interest'

- Does have such parental responsibilities or rights
- Has had, but no longer has parental responsibilities or rights (as a result of **private** law means e.g. under this section)

■ If the person has lost her/his parental responsibilities or rights as a result of adoption, freeing for adoption, a Parental Order under the HFEA 1990 or transferred to a local authority by a Parental Responsibility Order, s/he is excluded from making an application [s.11(4)]

*NB. The 'claiming an interest' provision permits the possibility of an application by a step-parent, **or** by 'civil partner' (i.e. same-sex couple who have registered their partnership under the Civil Partnership Act 2004).*

■ Alternatively, even though no application has been made, the court (even if it declines to make any other order) may make such an order [s.11 (3)].

NB. Subject to conditions contained in the Age of Legal Capacity (Scotland) Act, the child concerned may seek an order under s.11 but a local authority cannot [s.11 (5)].

■ In considering whether to make an order and which one to make, the court must:

- Regard the child's welfare as its paramount concern
- Not make any order unless it considers it would be better for the child than making no order at all and

- Take account of the child's age and maturity, where practicable providing her/him with an opportunity (if s/he wishes) to express her/his views and take account of views expressed [s.11(7)]

■ S.24 Family Law (Scotland) Act 2006 introduces the obligation for a court, in carrying out the above s.11(7) duties, to have regard in particular to the:

- Need to protect the child from any abuse (i.e. violence, harassment, threatening conduct and any other conduct giving rise or likely to give rise to physical or mental injury, fear alarm or distress; abuse of a person other than the child and domestic abuse) or risk of abuse which affects or might affect the child

NB. 'Conduct' includes speech and presence in a specified place or area

- Effect such abuse or risk of such abuse might have on the child
- Ability of a person who has carried out abuse which affects or might affect the child or might carry out such abuse to care for or otherwise meet the needs of the child and
- Effect any abuse, or the risk of any abuse might have on the carrying out of responsibilities in connection with the child's welfare by a person who has (or would have by virtue of s.11(1)) those responsibilities [s.11(7A) -7C)]

■ If the court is considering making an order under s.11(1) and 2 or more relevant persons (i.e. a person with parental responsibilities or rights in respect of the child or where a parent does not have parental responsibilities or parental rights, a parent of the child) would have to co-operate with one another as respects matters affecting the child:

- The court must consider whether it would be appropriate to make the order [s.11(7D);(7E)]

*NB. A child aged 12 or more is **presumed** to be of sufficient age and maturity to form a view in these circumstances [s.11 (10).*

Restrictions on Decrees for Divorce, Separation or Annulment Affecting Children [s.12 as amended by Civil Partnership Act 2004 Sch.28 para.60 & Sch2 para.8 Family Law (Scotland) Act 2006]

■ In any action for divorce, judicial separation or declarator of nullity of marriage (or dissolution or declarator of nullity of a civil partnership or separation of civil partners), the court must on the basis of the information about actual or proposed arrangements for the child's upbringing consider:

- Whether to exercise its powers to make an order under s.11 (orders relating to parental responsibilities etc) or s.54 (reference to the Principal Reporter) [s.12(1)]

- The court must postpone its decision about granting a decree if:

  - It is of the opinion that the circumstances of the case require, or are likely to require it to exercise any power under s.11 or s.54
  - It is not in a position to exercise that power without giving further consideration to the case; and
  - There are exceptional circumstances which make it desirable in the interests of that child that is should postpone its decision

NB. S.12 applies when the child is under 16 at the date on which the question first arises under s.12 (1) and a child of a civil partnership, means a child who has been accepted by both partners as a child of the family which their partnership constitutes [Sch.28 para.60 Civil Partnership Act 2004]

Part 2: Promotion of Children's Welfare by Local Authorities & Children's Hearings etc

Support for Children & Their Families

Introductory

Welfare of Child & Consideration of Her/ His Views [s.16]

■ In the circumstances of s.16(4) –summarised immediately below – a children's hearing or sheriff, taking account of the child's age and maturity, must so far as practicable:

- Give her/him an opportunity to indicate whether s/he wishes to express her/his views
- If s/he does so wish, provide the opportunity to express them and
- Have regard to such views as s/he may express [s.16(2)]

*NB. A child of 12 years of age or over must be **presumed** to be of sufficient age and maturity to form a view [s.16(2) (c)]*

■ The circumstances defined by s.16(4) are that:

- The children's hearing is considering whether to make or is reviewing a supervision requirement; whether to grant a warrant under s.66(1), s.69(4) or (7) or to provide under s.66(5) for the continuation of a warrant; is engaged in providing advice under s.60(10) or drawing up a report under s.73(13) **or**

- The sheriff is considering whether to make, vary or discharge a Parental Responsibilities Order, a Child Assessment Order or an Exclusion Order; to vary or discharge a Child Protection Order; to grant a s.67 warrant; in appeal to make such substitution as is mentioned in s.51(5)(c) (iii) or
- The sheriff is otherwise disposing of an appeal against a decision of a children's hearing [s.16(4)]

*NB. A children's hearing or court can determine that it will not afford paramountcy to the child's welfare if it considers this necessary in order to protect members of the public from **serious** harm (physical or not) [s.16(5)].*

Duty of Local Authority to Looked After Child [s.17]

■ Where a child is looked after by a local authority, it must:

- Safeguard and promote her/his welfare (which must be its paramount concern)
- Make such use of services available for children cared for by their own parents, as appears reasonable to the local authority
- Take such steps to promote, on a regular basis, personal relations and direct contact between the child and any person with parental responsibilities as appears (given the safeguarding duty) practicable and appropriate [s.17(1)]

■ The safeguarding duty includes a duty to provide advice and assistance with a view to preparing the child for when s/he is no longer looked after [s.17(2)]

■ Before making any decision with respect to a child it is looking after or proposing to look after, the local authority must so far as is reasonably practicable ascertain the views of:

- The child
- Her/his parents
- Anyone else who has parental rights in relation to her/him and
- Any other person whose views the authority consider relevant [s.17(3)]

■ In making any such decision, a local authority must so far as practicable have regard to:

- The views (if s/he wishes to express them) of the child concerned taking account age an maturity
- Such views as it has been able to ascertain of parents, others with parental rights or other relevant persons and
- The child's religious persuasion, racial origin and cultural and linguistic background [s.17(4)]

*NB. A local authority can determine it will not comply with the duties set out in s.17(1) if it considers this necessary to protect members of the public from **serious** harm (physical or not) [s.17(5)].*

Duty of Persons with Parental Responsibilities to Notify Change of Address [s.18]

■ When child is being looked after by a local authority, each natural person who has parental responsibilities in relation to the child, must without unreasonable delay, inform that authority whenever s/he changes her/his address [s.18(1)].

■ A person who knowingly fails to comply is liable on summary conviction to a level 1 fine (though it is a defence if the change was to the same address as that to which another person with parental responsibilities was changing and the accused had reasonable cause to believe the other person had informed the authority [s.18 (2)].

Provision of Services

Local Authority Children's Services Plan [s.19]

■ Local authorities have an obligation to prepare, publish and from time to time, review plans for their provision, of relevant services (e.g. disabled children, provision of accommodation, day care and after care and training) to children in their area [s.19 (1);(2);(3)].

■ In preparing any plan or carrying out any review, the local authority must consult:

• Every health board and NHS trust providing services in the area of the authority

- Such voluntary organisations as appear to the authority to represent the interests of users or potential service users, or to provide services in the area that might be categorised as 'relevant services' if the local authority provided them
- The Principal Reporter appointed under s.127 Local Government etc (Scotland) Act 1994
- Chairperson of the children's panel for that area
- Such housing associations, voluntary housing agencies and other bodies as appear to the authority to provide housing in that area and
- Others as the Secretary of State may direct [s.19(5)]

Publication of Information about Services for Children [s.20]

■ A local authority must prepare and publish information about 'relevant services' (defined in s.19) in its area:

- It or another local authority provides or
- Where considered appropriate, about services the local authority has the power to provide itself, but which are being provided by voluntary organisations or other persons [s.20 (10).

Co-operation between Authorities [s.21]

■ When it appears to a local authority that the following persons could help in the exercise of any of their functions under Part 11, it may specify the things required and ask for their help:

- Any other local authority
- A health board
- A national health service trust
- Any other person authorised by the Secretary of State

■ Appropriate persons receiving such a request must comply with it provided that it is compatible with their own statutory or other duties and obligations and (in the case of organisations) does not unduly prejudice the discharge of any of their functions [s.21(1)].

Promotion of Welfare of Children in Need [s.22]

■ A local authority must safeguard and promote the welfare of children in its area who are in need, and so far as is consistent with that duty, promote the upbringing of such children by their families, by providing a range and level of services appropriate to the children's needs [s.22(1)].

■ In providing those services, the local authority must have regard, so far as practicable to each child's religious persuasion, racial origin and cultural and linguistic background [s.22(2)].

■ A service may:

- Be provided for a particular child
- Be provided for her/his or a member of the family if done with a view to safeguarding or promoting her/his welfare and

- Include giving assistance in kind or in exceptional circumstances, in cash [s.22(3)]

NB. Assistance may be given unconditionally or subject to conditions as to repayment in whole or in part of its value though the local authority must before giving it or imposing conditions have regard to the means of the child/family concerned and cannot require repayment at any time of a person when in receipt of income support or working families tax credit, any element of child tax credit other than the family element or working tax credit or an income-based jobseeker's allowance [s.22(4)].

Children Affected by Disability [s.23]

- Services provided by a local authority must be designed to:

  - Minimise the effect on any disabled child within the authority's area of her/his disability, as well minimise the impact of a family member's disability on a child
  - Give those children the opportunity to lead as normal lives as possible [s.23(1)]

  NB. For the purposes of ss.16–38, a person is 'disabled' if chronically sick or disabled or has a mental disorder (as defined in s.328(1) Mental Health (Care and Treatment) (Scotland) Act 2003

- When requested to do so by a child's parent or guardian a local authority must in order to discharge its s.22(1) duty to promote the welfare of children:

- Carry out an assessment of the child or of any other person in the child's family to determine the needs of the child in so far as attributable to her/his disability or to that of another person [s.22(3)]

■ In determining the needs of a child, the local authority must take account:

- When it appears to the authority that a 'carer' provides a substantial amount of care on a regular basis for the child, or for another person in the child's family who is being assessed under s.23(3), of such care as is being provided and
- In so far as reasonable and practicable to do so, of the views of parent/guardian and child and the views of the carer, providing that they have a wish or capacity to express a view [s.23(4)]

Assessment of Ability of Carers to Provide Care for Disabled Children [s.24]

■ A carer (child or adult) who provides or intends to provide a substantial amount of care on a regular basis for a disabled child, may request a local authority to undertake a 'carer's assessment' of her/his ability to provide or continue to provide such care [s.24 (1)].

■ The local authority to which the request is made must:

- Where it appears to it that the child or another person in her/his family is a person for whom it must or may provide services under s.22(1) comply with the request and

- If it then or subsequently makes an assessment under s.23(3) to determine the child's needs it must have regard to the results of the carer's assessment both in the assessment of the child and in making a decision as to discharge of any duty under s.2(1) Chronically Sick and Disabled Persons Act 1970 or under s.22 of this Act

NB. No request may be made under s.24 (1) by a person who provides/will provide the care in question on a commercial or voluntary basis [s.24 (2)].

■ When it appears to a local authority both that a child is disabled and is or may be entitled to s.24 services, and that a carer provides or intends to provide a substantial amount of care on a regular basis:

- The local authority must notify the carer s/he may be entitled under s.24(1) to request an assessment of her/his ability to provide/continue to provide care for the child [s.24A as inserted by the Community Care and Health (Scotland) Act 2002]

Provision of Accommodation for Children etc [s.25]

■ The local authority must provide accommodation for a child within its area for whom nobody has parental responsibility, who is lost/abandoned or when, for any reason, the ordinary caregiver is prevented from providing suitable accommodation or care [s.25 (1)].

NB. A local authority providing accommodation under s.25(1) for a child ordinarily resident in another authority, must notify in writing, the other authority, who may then take over at any time, its provision of accommodation [s.25(4)].

■ The local authority may also provide accommodation to any child within its area if it considers that to do would safeguard or promote her/his welfare [s.25 (2)].

■ A local authority may provide accommodation for those 18–20 inclusive if it considers it would safeguard or promote the young person's welfare [s.25 (3)].

■ A local authority providing accommodation under s.25(1) for a child ordinarily resident in another local authority, must notify the other authority in writing and that other authority may at any time take over the provision of accommodation for the child [s.25(4)].

■ Before providing accommodation under s.25, a local authority must have regard, so far as is practicable, to her/his views (if expressed) taking account of age and maturity and a child aged 12 or over is presumed to be of sufficient age and maturity to form a view [s.25 (5)].

Removal from Accommodation [s.25 (6) ;(7)]

■ Anyone with parental responsibility or rights to control residence or direct or guide (as in s.2 (1) (a) ;(b) may remove a child from accommodation unless s/he is 16 or 17 and disagrees.

■ Effective agreements with parents should reduce potential problems but if 'significant harm' appears likely, emergency protection measures are available.

■ A holder of a Residence Order can authorise the retention of a child in accommodation in spite of a parent's wishes to remove.

NB. The power of a person who has parental responsibility and who is willing and able to provide accommodation to remove the child from accommodation is moderated if the child has been accommodated by one or more authorities for a continuous period of 6 months. In such cases, 14 days notice is required [s.25 (7)].

Manner of Provision of Accommodation [s.26]

■ A local authority may provide accommodation for a child by:

- Placing her/him with a family, relative or other suitable person
- Maintaining her/him in a residential establishment
- Making other suitable arrangements including use of local services [s.26(1)]

Day Care for Pre-School & Other Children [s.27]

■ Each local authority must provide such day care for children in need aged 5 and less and not yet at school, as is appropriate and may also provide such day care for those not in need [s.27(1)].

■ A local authority may provide facilities (including training, advice, guidance and counselling) for those caring for children in day care or who at any time accompany such children [s.27(2)].

■ Each local authority is also obliged to provide for children in need within its area who attend school, as is appropriate, care outside school hours and during school holidays (and may do so for those not in need) [s.27(3)].

NB. Day care in s.27 means any from of care provided for children during the day whether or not provided on a regular basis [s.27 (4)].

Advice & Assistance for Young Persons Formerly Looked After by Local Authorities

After Care [s.29]

■ A local authority must, unless satisfied the young person's welfare does not require it:

• Advise, guide and assist any person its area over school age and under 19, who was when s/he ceased to be of school age or subsequently became but is no longer looked after by a local authority [s.29(1)]

■ A local authority has the discretion to provide advice, guidance and assistance to those aged 19 or 20, no longer looked after by local authority and who request such help [s.29 (2)].

NB. Assistance given under either of the above provisions may include assistance in kind or in cash [s.29 (3)].

For the purposes of s.19, looked after by a local authority includes those who have been looked after in England or Wales as well as Scotland [s.29 (7)].

■ Each local authority must, in relation to those entitled to receive or request services under the above provisions, carry out an assessment of the individual's needs [s.29(5)].

■ When a person over school age ceases to be looked after by a local authority or is being helped under s.29(1) or s.29(2) as above and proposes to reside in another authority:

- The local authority must, subject to the young person's consent, inform the other authority [s.29(4)]

■ Each local authority must establish a procedure for considering representations (including complaints) made to it by those mentioned in s.29(1) and s.29(2) about its assessment or provision of services to the specified care leavers [s.29(6)].

Financial Assistance towards Expenses of Education & Training [s.30]

■ A local authority may make:

- Grants to any 'relevant person' in its area to enable her/him to meet expenses connected with education/training and
- Contributions to her/his accommodation and maintenance in any place where the young person is employed/seeking employment/receiving education or training [s.30(1)]

■ For the above purposes, a 'relevant person' is someone who:

- Is over school age but not yet 21 and
- At the time when s/he ceased to be of school age or any subsequent time was, but is no longer looked after by a local authority [s.30(2)]

NB. Grants and contributions can be continued after the person reaches 21 until her/his education/ training is completed, though any interruption of education/training after s/he reaches 21 removes the local authority's power to assist unless the course is recommended as soon as is practicable [s.30(3)].

Miscellaneous & General

Review Duties [s.31]

■ It is the duty of each local authority which is looking after a child to review her/his case at regular intervals as specified by the Secretary of State in regulations.

NB. The relevant regulations are the 'Arrangements to Look After Children (Scotland) Regulations 1996 (SI 1996/3262 and Children (Scotland) Act 1995 etc (Revocations and Savings) (Scotland) Regulations 1997 (SI 1997/691).

Removal of a Child from Residential Establishment [s.32]

■ A local authority, regardless of any agreement it may have made about the placement:

• May at any time remove a child from a residential establishment and
• Must do so if asked to do so by the person responsible for the establishment

Welfare of Certain Children in Hospitals and Nursing Homes etc [s.36]

■ When a child is being accommodated by a health board, NHS trust, private hospital or care home and the person providing the accommodation concludes that the child has not been visited personally by anyone who has parental responsibility for more

than 3 months, that person must inform the local
authority [s.36(1)].

■ The local authority must then determine whether the
child's welfare is adequately safeguarded and
promoted and whether it needs to exercise any of its
functions under this Act [s.36(2)].

Short-term Refuges for Children at Risk of Harm [s.38]

■ If a child appears to a local authority to be at risk of
harm and the child requests it, the authority may, for
a period of up to 7 – and exceptionally as prescribed
by the Secretary of State 14 days):

• Provide her/him with refuge in a residential
establishment it controls or manages or one it
designates for this purpose or

• Arrange for a person whose household is
'approved' under s.5(3)(b) Social Work (Scotland)
Act 1968 to provide her/him with refuge
[s.38(1)(a)]

■ Where a child appears to a person
providing/managing/employed in the management
of a care home to be at risk of harm, that person
may, at the child's request provide refuge in that
accommodation for a period of up to 7 – and in
exceptional circumstances prescribed by the
Secretary of State 14 days)

*NB. Refuge may only be provided as above if and to
the extent that, the local authority within whose area*

the establishment is situated gives its approval [s.38 (1) (b)].

■ While a child is being provided with refuge under s.38 s/he is not to be regarded as a foster child, nor do the following legal provisions apply:

- Offences in relation to parental responsibilities orders as per s.89 (and so far as it relates to anything done in Scotland, s.83)
- Compelling, persuading, inciting or assisting anyone to be absent from detention contrary to s.32(3) Children and Young Persons Act 1969 [s.38(3);(4)]

Children's Hearings

Constitution of Children's Hearings

NB. The Children's Services (Scotland) Bill 2007 proposes a significant number of changes to the current arrangements for children's hearings.

Formation of Children's Panel & Children's Hearings [s.39]

■ In each local government area, there must be a children's panel for the purposes of the Children (Scotland) Act 1995 and other related legislation [s.39 (1)].

NB. Sch. 1 specifies requirements with respect to the recruitment, appointment, training and expenses of panel members as well as the establishment of a panel advisory committee [s.39 (2)].

■ 'Children's hearings' are to be constituted so that there are 3 members, at least one of whom is male and at least one female and one of the members must chair the hearing [s.39(5)].

Qualification & employment of reporters

Qualification & Employment of Reporters [s.40]

■ The qualifications of a reporter are prescribed in regulation by the Secretary of State.

■ A reporter must not, unless/she has the consent of the Scottish Children's Reporter Administration, be employed by a local authority.

Safeguards for children

Safeguarding Child's Interests in Proceedings [s.41]

■ In any ss.39–51 or protection and supervision proceedings, at a children's hearing or before the sheriff, the hearing/sheriff :

- Must consider if it is necessary to appoint a person to safeguard the interests of the child in the proceedings and
- If so, must appoint on such terms and conditions as appear appropriate [s.41(1)] and
- Must state the reasons for the decision made [s.41(3)]

NB. The above provision does not apply to a Child Protection Order under s.57 [s.41 (2)].

■ The expenses of a person appointed to safeguard a child so far as reasonably incurred in safeguarding the interests of the child (and unless defrayed in terms of regulations made under s.101) must be borne by the local authority:

- For whose area the panel from which the relevant hearing has been constituted, has been formed or,

- When there is no relevant hearing e.g. the safeguarder has been appointed by the sheriff, within whose area the child resides [s.41(4)]

NB. A relevant hearing means in the case of proceedings at a children's hearing, that hearing; under s.68 the hearing who have directed the application and on an appeal against s.51, he hearing whose decision is being appealed against [s.41(5)].

Conduct of proceedings at and in connection with children's hearing

Power of Secretary of State to Make Rules Governing Procedures at Children's Hearing etc [s.42]

- The Children's Hearings (Transmission of Information) etc (Scotland) Regulations 1996, Children's Hearings (Scotland) Rules 1996 and the Children's Hearings (Scotland) Rules 1986 (Revocations) (Scotland) Rules 1997 provide rules for constituting and arranging children's hearings and other meetings of members of the panel and its procedure and cover:

  - Conduct and potential scope of business meetings convened under s.64
  - Notification of the time and place of the children's hearing to the child and relevant others
  - How the grounds for referring the case to a children's hearing under s.65(1) are to be stated,

and the rights of the child and relevant others to dispute those grounds

- The Principal Reporter, making available, subject to conditions, reports/information s/he receives to panel members, any child concerned, and any others relevant persons or specified class of persons
- The safeguarding procedure under s.41
- The functions of a 'safeguarder' appointed under s.41(1) and any right s/he has to information about the proceedings in question
- The recording in writing of any statement given under s.41(3)
- The right to appeal to the sheriff under s.51(1)(a) against a decision of the children's hearing and notification arrangements
- The right of the child and any relevant person to be represented at the hearing
- The entitlement of the child, relevant person and any representative they may have to the refund of expenses incurred in consequence of the hearing
- Persons who are allowed to attend a children's hearing

Privacy of Proceedings & Right to Attend Children's Hearing [s.43]

■ A children's hearing must be conducted in private and members of the public are not allowed to attend [s.43 (1)].

- The chairperson must take all reasonable steps to ensure that the number of persons present at a children's hearing at any one time is kept to a minimum [s.43 (2)].

- A member of the Council of Tribunals or of the Scottish Committee of that Council and (subject to the conditions of s.43 (4) below) a journalist have the right to attend a children's hearing [s.43 (3)].

- A children's hearing may exclude a journalist from any part/s of the hearing where and for so long as it is satisfied that:

  - It is necessary to do so in the interests of the child so as to obtain her/his views or
  - The presence of the journalist is causing or is likely to cause significant distress to the child [s.43(4)]

  NB. Where a children's hearing has exercised the power to exclude a journalist, the chairperson may, at the end of that exclusion offer a summary of what has taken place [s.43 (5)].

Prohibition of Publication of Proceedings at Children's Hearing [s.44 as amended]

- S.44 prohibits the publication of any matter intended or likely to identify a child, her/his address or school, whose case:

  - Has been referred to a reporter
  - Is subject to proceedings at a children's hearing

- Is before a sheriff in relation to child protection or exclusion orders, referrals from a children's hearing, re-hearing of evidence or an appeal [s.44(1)]

NB. Any person who contravenes s.44(1) is liable on summary conviction to a fine of up to level 4 on the standard scale for each contravention [s.44(2)]

Attendance of Child & Relevant Person at Children's Hearing [s.45]

■ s.44 obliges the child and relevant person to attend the hearing and makes it a criminal offence if the relevant person does not do so. It also provides for the issuing of warrants to find, keep and bring a child to the children's hearing.

■ The child who has been notified of the fact that a hearing has been arranged either to put the grounds of a referral to her/him; to discuss established grounds or to review an existing supervision requirement, **has a right and is obliged** to attend all stages of the hearing [s.45(1)].

■ The children's hearing may though, conduct all or any part of the proceedings without the child if s/he chooses not to attend and the hearing decide to release her/him from her/his obligation [s.45 (2)].

■ The Principal Reporter is responsible for securing the attendance of the child at the first any subsequent hearing [s.45 (3)].

- When the Reporter believes that a child is unlikely to attend a hearing due, s/he may apply to the Children's Hearing who may issue a warrant to:

  - Find the child
  - Keep her/him in a place of safety and
  - Bring her/him before the children's hearing [s.45(4)]

- Where a child has failed to attend a children's hearing in accordance with notice issued under s.45(1), the hearing may on the application of the Principal Reporter or of its own motion, issue a warrant which has the same effect as one issued under s.45(4) above [s.45(5)].

- A child who has been taken to a place of safety under a s.45 warrant must not be kept there more than whichever is the earlier of:

  - 7 days from being taken to the place of safety or
  - The day on which the children's hearing first sits [s.45(6)]

- Where a child has been **found,** in pursuance of a warrant and cannot immediately be brought before a children's hearing, the Principal Reporter must wherever practicable arrange a hearing to sit on the first working day thereafter [s.45(7)].

- Unless excluded from the hearing under s.46 [see below], a 'relevant person' (defined in s.93(2)(b) as a parent with parental responsibilities or rights or another person vested with such responsibilities or rights or anyone else who appears to ordinarily have charge or control over the child):

- Has the right to attend all stages of the hearing
- Is obliged to attend at all stages unless the hearing is satisfied it would be unreasonable to require her/his attendance or that it is not necessary for the proper consideration of the case [s.45(8)]

NB. Any person who fails to meet the above obligation is liable on summary conviction to a fine not exceeding level 3 on the standard scale [s.45(9)].

Power to Exclude Relevant Person from Children's Hearing [s.46]

■ When a children's hearing is considering the case of a child, it has the discretion to exclude a 'relevant person' (defined above) and/or her/his representative/s from any parts of the hearing for so long as is necessary in the child's interests, where it is satisfied that:

- It must do so in order to obtain the views of the child in relation to the case or
- The presence of the person/s in question is causing or is likely to cause significant distress to the child [s.46(1)]

NB. A relevant person can be excluded as above, only at the stage at which the grounds are being put i.e. not at the stage at which the case itself is being considered.

■ When a children's hearing exercises the power to exclude under s.46(1), the chairperson **must**, after the exclusion has ended, explain to any excluded person the substance of what took place in her/his absence [s.46(2)].

Presumption & Determination of Age [s.47]

■ When a children's hearing has been arranged in respect of any person, the hearing:

  • **Must** at the commencement of the proceedings enquire as to the age of that person and proceed with the hearing only if s/he declares she is a 'child' or the hearing determines this is so and

  • **May**, at any time before the conclusion of the proceedings, accept a declaration by the child or make a fresh determination as to her/his age [s.47(1)]

■ A 'child' for this purpose is a child:

  • Under 16 years of age
  • Of 16 or 17 who has a supervision requirement in force
  • Whose case has been referred to a children's hearing from another part of the UK (where childhood extends to 18)
  • Over 16 but still of school age, and referred on the ground of non-school attendance [s.93(2)]

■ The declared or determined age is, for the purposes of this Act to be considered the true age of that person [s.47 (2)].

NB. No decision reached, order continued, warrant granted or requirement imposed by a children's hearing is invalidated by any subsequent proof that the age of the person had not been correctly declared or determined [s.47(3)].

Transfer etc of Cases

Transfer of Case to Another Children's Hearing [s.48]

■ Where a children's hearing is satisfied that in relation to a case it is hearing, that it would be better considered by a hearing in a different local government area, it may at any time during the course of its hearing request the Principal Reporter to arrange for another children's hearing to dispose of the case [s.48(1)].

■ Accepted or established grounds remain accepted or established before the new hearing [s.48 (2)].

Treatment of Child's Case on Remission by Court [s.50]

■ When a court has under s.49 Criminal Procedure (Scotland) Act 1995, has remitted a case to a children's hearing for disposal, a certificate signed by the clerk of the court stating that the child/young person concerned has pled guilty or has been found guilty of the offence to which the remit relates, is conclusive evidence for the purpose of remit, that the offence **has** been committed by the child/young person [s.50 (1)].

■ The provisions of the Children (Scotland) Act 1995 apply to a child thus remitted even if s/he is aged 16 or 17 and would otherwise not be considered a child [s.50(2)].

Appeals

Appeals Against Decision of Children's Hearing or Sheriff [s.51]

■ Decisions of the children's hearing or of the sheriff can be appealed against by the child or relevant person.

■ An appeal about any decision of the children's hearing is to the sheriff.

■ An appeal about any decision of the sheriff (on an application for finding established a ground of referral or in dealing with an appeal from the hearing's decision) can be appealed to the Sheriff Principal and then to the Court of Session if on a point of law or about a procedural irregularity.

Protection & Supervision of Children

Children Requiring Compulsory Measures of Supervision

Children Requiring Compulsory Measures of Supervision [s.52(1) as amended]

■ The question of whether compulsory measures of supervision are necessary in respect of a child arises if at least 1 of the conditions in s.52 (2) below is satisfied [s.52 (1)].

NB. A children's hearing cannot consider the case of a child to determine whether compulsory measures of supervision are required unless 1 or more of those conditions has been accepted, or proved to exist.

■ The conditions are that the child:

- Is beyond the control of any relevant person
- Is falling into bad association or is exposed to moral danger
- Is likely – due to lack of parental care, to suffer unnecessarily or be impaired seriously in health or development
- Is a child in respect of whom any of the offences mentioned in Sch.1 Criminal Procedure (Scotland) Act 1995 i.e. offences against children to which special measures apply, has been committed
- Is, or is likely to become a member of the same household as a child in respect of whom any of the above Sch.1 offences has been committed

- Is , or is likely to become a member of the same household as a person who has committed any of the above Sch.1 offences
- Is, or is likely to become a member of the same household as a person in respect of whom an offence under ss. 1–3 Criminal Law (Consolidation) (Scotland) 1995 i.e. incest and intercourse with a child by step-parent or person in position of trust – has been committed by a member of that household
- Has failed to attend school regularly without reasonable cause
- Has committed an offence
- Has misused alcohol or any drug ('controlled' within the meaning of the Misuse of Drugs Act 1971 or not)
- Has misused a volatile substance by deliberately inhaling its vapour, other than for medicinal purposes
- Is being provided with accommodation by a local authority under s.25 or is subject of a s.86 Parental Responsibilities Order – and in either case her/his behaviour is such that special measures are necessary for her/his adequate supervision in the interests of self or others [s.52(2)]

NB. In Part 2, 'supervision' in relation to compulsory measures of supervision may include measures taken for the protection, guidance, treatment or control of the child [s.52 (3)].

Preliminary & Investigatory Measures

Provision of Information to the Principal Reporter [s.53]

■ Where information is received by a local authority which **suggests** that compulsory measures of supervision may be necessary in respect of a child, it must:

- Cause inquiries to be made unless it is satisfied that such inquiries are unnecessary
- (If it appears to it after such inquiries, or after being satisfied that such inquiries are unnecessary) that such measures may be required, give to the Principal Reporter such information about the child as it has been able to discover [s.53(1)]

■ A person, other than a local authority who has **reasonable cause to believe** that compulsory measures of supervision may be necessary in respect of a child:

- **Must** (if s/he is a police officer) give to the Principal Reporter such information about the child as it has been able to discover and
- In any other case, **may** do so [s.53(2)]

NB. There is no restriction on which members of the public (including the child her/himself) or which professionals are able to pass information to the Reporter.

■ In circumstances where the police have a duty to make a report about the commission of offences to the appropriate prosecutor (s.17 (1) Police (Scotland) Act 1967), in relation to a child, they must also make a report to the Principal Reporter [s.53 (3)].

NB. 'In relation to a child' means the child may have been victim or perpetrator.

■ When an application has been made to the sheriff by the Principal Reporter in accordance with directions given by a children's hearing under s.65(7) or s.65(9), or by any person entitled to make an application under s.85:

• The Principal Reporter may request any prosecutor to supply her/him with any evidence lawfully obtained in the course of, and held by the prosecutor in connection with the investigation of a crime or suspected crime if it might assist the sheriff in determining the application (and subject to s.53(5), it is the duty of the prosecutor to comply with such a request [s.53(4)]

■ A prosecutor may refuse to comply with a request issued under s.53(4) where s/he reasonably believes that it is necessary to retain the evidence for the purposes of any of her/his current or intended criminal proceedings [s.53(5)]

NB. The Lord Advocate may direct that in any specified case or class of cases, any evidence lawfully obtained in the course of an investigation of a crime or suspected crime must be supplied without the need for a request under s.53(4) to the Principal Reporter [s.53(6)].

Reference to the Principal Reporter by Court [s.54]

■ In any 'relevant proceedings', where it appears to the court that the following s.52(2) conditions are satisfied with respect to a child, the court may refer and specify matter to the Principal Reporter. The conditions are that the child:

- Is beyond the control of any relevant person
- Is falling into bad association or is exposed to moral danger
- Is likely – due to lack of parental care, to suffer unnecessarily or be impaired seriously in health or development
- Is a child in respect of whom any of the offences mentioned in Sch.1 Criminal Procedure (Scotland) Act 1995 i.e. offences against children to which special measures apply, has been committed
- Is, or is likely to become a member of the same household as a child in respect of whom any of the above Sch.1 offences has been committed
- Is , or is likely to become a member of the same household as a person who has committed any of the above Sch.1 offences
- Is, or is likely to become a member of the same household as a person in respect of whom an

offence under ss. 1–3 Criminal Law
(Consolidation) (Scotland) 1995 i.e. incest and
intercourse with a child by step-parent or person
in position of trust – has been committed by a
member of that household

- Has failed to attend school regularly without
  reasonable cause
- Has misused alcohol or any drug ('controlled'
  within the meaning of the Misuse of Drugs Act
  1971 or not)
- Has misused a volatile substance by deliberately
  inhaling its vapour, other than for medicinal
  purposes
- Is being provided with accommodation by a
  local authority under s.25 or is subject of a s.86
  Parental Responsibilities Order – and in either
  case her/his behaviour is such that special
  measures are necessary for her/his adequate
  supervision in the interests of self or others
  [s.52(2)]

■ 'Relevant proceedings' in s.54 means:

- An action for divorce, judicial separation, or for
  declarator of marriage, nullity of marriage,
  parentage or non-parentage
- Proceedings relating to parental responsibilities
  or parental rights under Part 1 of this Act
- Proceedings for an Adoption or Freeing Order
  under the Adoption (Scotland) Act 1978
- Proceedings for an offence against s.35 (failure
  by parent to secure regular attendance of

her/his child at school), s.41(failure to comply with an attendance order) of the Education (Scotland) Act 1980 [s.54(2)]

■ On receipt of a referral under s.54(1) the Principal Reporter must make such investigations as s/he thinks appropriate and:

- **If** s/he considers that compulsory measures of supervision are necessary, arrange a children's hearing to consider the case of a child under s.69 [s.54(3)]

NB. The grounds will be treated as per s.68 as being established by the sheriff, thus if a hearing is convened, it will not need to put the ground of referral to the child or parent.

Child Assessment Orders (CAO) [s.55]

Application for CAO

■ A sheriff may, on the application of a local authority grant a CAO for an assessment of the child's health or development, or of the way in which s/he has been treated, if s/he is satisfied that:

- The local authority has reasonable cause to suspect that the child is being so treated or neglected that s/he is suffering or likely to suffer significant harm
- Such assessment is required to establish whether or not there is reasonable cause to believe that the child is so treated or neglected and

- • Such assessment is unlikely to be carried out or carried out satisfactorily unless the order is granted [s.55(1)]

- ■ When an application has been made for a CAO and the sheriff considers that the conditions for making a Child Protection Order under s.57 are satisfied, s/he must make the Child Protection Order as if the application by the local authority was under s.57 [s.55(2)].

Effect of CAO

- ■ A CAO must:

  - • Specify the date on which it is to begin
  - • Have effect for such period as specified in the order to a maximum of 7 days
  - • Require any person in a position to do so to produce her/him to any authorised person; to permit that person or any other authorised person to carry out an assessment in accordance with the order and comply with any other conditions of the order and
  - • Be carried out by an authorised person in accordance with the terms of the order [s.55(3)]

  NB. In s.55 an authorised person means any officer of the local authority and any person authorised by the local authority to perform any or all of the assessment [s.55 (6)].

- A CAO may:
  - When necessary, permit the taking of the child concerned to any place for the purpose of the assessment and
  - Authorise the child to be kept at that place, or any other place, for such period of time as may be specified in the order [s.55(4)]

- When a CAO makes provisions under s.55(4) above, it must contain such directions as the sheriff considers appropriate as to the contact which the child is to be allowed with any other person whilst s/he is in any place to which s/he has been taken/is being kept under the order [s.55(5)].

Initial Investigation by the Principal Reporter

- When the Principal Reporter receives information from any source about a case which may require a children's hearing to be arranged, s/he must after such initial investigation as s/he thinks necessary proceed as follows [s.56(1)].

  NB. For the purposes of making any initial investigation under s.56 (1), the Principal Reporter may request from the local authority a report on the child and relevant circumstances. The local authority must supply the report which may contain such information from any person as the Principal Reporter or the local authority think fit [s.56(2)].

The above report may contain information additional to that given by the local authority under s.53 [s.56(3)].

■ The Principal Reporter may decide, after an initial investigation that a children's hearing does not need to be arranged and if s/he so decides:

- Must inform the child, any relevant person and the person who brought the case to her/his notice (or any of those persons) and
- May, if s/he considers it appropriate, refer the case to a local authority with a view to it making arrangements for advice, guidance and assistance of the child and her/his family [s.56(4)]

■ When it appears to the Principal Reporter that compulsory measures of supervision are necessary in respect of the child, s/he must arrange a children's hearing and refer the case for consideration and determination [s.56(6)].

NB. When the Principal Reporter has arranged a children's hearing on accordance with s.56(6), s/he must (unless already done) request a report and may request the local authority such information, supplementary or additional as s/he thinks fit ands the local authority must supply that report and/such information as it considers relevant [s.56(7)]

■ When the Principal Reporter has decided that a children's hearing does **not** need to be arranged, s/he must not retract the decision unless new and additional circumstances arise [s.56 (5)].

Measures for the Emergency Protection of Children

Child Protection Orders (CPOs) [s.57]

Application for CPO

- A sheriff may make a CPO when, on the application of a person, s/he is satisfied that there are reasonable grounds to believe that a child:

  - Is being so treated or neglected that s/he is suffering significant harm, **or** will suffer such if not removed to and kept in a place of safety, or if s/he does not remain in the place s/he is being accommodated (whether or not resident) and
  - A CPO is necessary to protect that child from such harm/further harm [s.57(1)]

- A sheriff may also make a CPO when, on the application of a local authority, s/he is satisfied that:

  - The local authority has reasonable grounds to suspect that a child is being or will be so treated or neglected that s/he is suffering or will suffer significant harm
  - It is making or causing to be made enquiries to allow the authority to decide whether it should take any action to safeguard the child's welfare and
  - Those enquiries are being frustrated by unreasonable denial of access to the child (when the authority has reasonable cause to believe

that such access is required as a matter of urgency) [s.57(2)]

- In addition to the rules introduced under s.91 Act of Sedurunt (Family Proceedings in the Sheriff Court) SI 1996/2167, an application for a CPO must:

  - Identify the applicant
  - So far as practicable, identify the child for whom the order is ought
  - State the grounds for the application and
  - Be accompanied by such supporting evidence (documentary or otherwise) as will enable the sheriff to determine the application [s.57(3)]

Effect of CPO

- A CPO may, subject to such terms and conditions as the sheriff considers appropriate, do any one or more of the following:

  - Require any person in a position to do so, to produce the child to the applicant
  - Authorise the removal of the child by the applicant to a place of safety, and the keeping of the child at that place
  - Authorise the prevention of the removal of the child from any place where s/he is being accommodated
  - Provide that the location of any place of safety in which the child is being kept should not be disclosed to any person or class of person specified in the order [s.57(4)]

■ In taking any action required or permitted by a CPO or in a s.58 direction (see below), the applicant must only act where/she reasonably believes that to so is necessary to safeguard or promote the welfare of the child [s.57 (6)].

NB. When the local authority provides a place of safety for a child removed on a CPO, it has (subject to terms and conditions of the order) the same duties as it would toward a looked after child under s.17[s.57(7)].

Directions in Relation to Contact & Exercise of Parental Responsibilities & Rights [s.58]

■ When the sheriff makes a CPO, s/he must at that time consider whether it is necessary to give a direction to the applicant for the order as to contact with the child for any:

- Parent of the child
- Person with parental responsibilities in relation to the child and
- Other specified person or class of persons

■ If s/he determines that there is such a necessity s/he may give such a direction [s.58 (1)].

■ A direction under s.58(1) may:

- Prohibit contact with the child for any persons mentioned in that subsection;
- Make contact with the child for any person subject to such conditions as the sheriff

considers appropriate to safeguard and promote the welfare of the child [s.58(2)]

NB. Such directions may make different provision in relation to different persons or classes of persons [s.58 (3)].

■ A person applying for a CPO under s.57 (1) or (2) may at the same time apply to the sheriff for a direction in relation to the exercise or fulfilment of any parental responsibilities or parental rights in respect of the child concerned, if the person considers such a direction necessary to safeguard or promote the welfare of the child [s.58 (4)].

■ Such directions under s.68(4) may be sought in relation to any examination as to the physical or mental state of the child, any other assessment or interview of the child or any treatment of the child arising out of such an examination or assessment, which is to be carried out by any person [s.58(5)].

NB. The sheriff may give a direction sought under s.58(4) where s/he considers is in necessary; and such a direction may be granted subject to such conditions, if any, as s/he (having regard in particular to the duration of the CPO to which it relates) considers appropriate [s.58(6)].

■ A s.58 direction ceases to have effect when the:

- Sheriff, on an application under s.60(7), directs that it is cancelled; or the
- CPO to which it relates ceases to have effect [s.58(7)]

Initial Hearing [s.59]

■ S.59 applies when:

- A child subject to a CPO has been taken to a place of safety or is prevented from being removed from any place
- The Principal Reporter has not exercised her/his powers under s.60(3) to discharge the child from the place of safety and
- The Principal Reporter has not received notice, in accordance with s.60(9), of an application under s.60 (7) [s.59(1)]

■ In this case, the Principal Reporter must arrange a children's hearing to conduct an initial hearing of the child's case in order to determine whether they should, in the interests of the child, continue the Child Protection Order under s.59(4) [s.59(2)].

NB. A children's hearing arranged under s.59 (2) above must take place on the 2nd working day after that order is implemented [s.59 (3)].

■ When a children's hearing arranged under s.59 (2) above is satisfied that the conditions for the making of a CPO are established, it may continue the order and any direction given under s.58 (with or without variation of the order or, as the case may be, the direction) until the commencement of a children's hearing in relation to the child arranged in accordance with s.65 (2) [s.59 (4)].

*NB. Any reference, in relation to calculation of any period, to the time at which a child protection order is implemented is a reference (where relevant) to the day on which the child was removed to a place of safety in accordance **or** (when relevant) to authorisation of the prevention of her/his removal from a specified place. In the former case, 'implementation' occurs on the day of removal; in the latter, the day or the order [s.59 (5)].*

Duration, Recall or Variation of a CPO [s.60]

- Where, by the end of 24 hours of a CPO being made (other than one authorising prevention of a child's removal from a place in which s/he is being accommodated), the applicant has made no attempt to implement the order, it will cease to have effect [s.60 (1)].

- When an application made under s.60 (7) below has not been determined in accordance with s.60 (8) below, the order to which the application relates will cease to have effect [s.60(2)].

- When the Principal Reporter, having regard to the welfare of the child, considers that (as a result of a change in the circumstances or of further information by her/him) the conditions for making a CPO are no longer satisfied or that the term/condition/direction is no longer appropriate, and notifies the person who implemented the order that s/he so considers, then a child cannot be:

- Kept in a place of safety under a CPO
- Prevented from being removed from any place by such an order or
- Subject to any term or condition contained in such an order or a direction given under s.58 [s.60(3)]

■ The Principal Reporter must not give notice under s.60(3) above where:

- Proceedings before a children's hearing arranged under s.59(2) have commenced; or
- The hearing of an application made under s.60(7) has begun [s.60(4)]

■ When the Principal Reporter has given notice under s.60 (3) above, s/he must also, in such manner as may be prescribed, notify the sheriff who made the order [s.60 (5)].

■ A CPO ceases to have effect where:

- An initial hearing arranged does not continue the order as described above
- An application is made to the sheriff under s.60 (7) on the sheriff recalling such order under s.60 (13)
- The person who implemented the order receives notice from the Principal Reporter that s/he has decided not to refer the case of a child to a children's hearing
- The Principal Reporter gives notice in accordance with s.60(3) that s/he considers the conditions for the making of it are no longer satisfied or where

- Such an order is continued by the hearing or sheriff respectively on commencement of a children's hearing arranged under s.65(2) [s.60(6)]

■ An application to the sheriff to set aside or vary a CPO made under s.57 or a direction under s.58 or such an order or direction continued (with or without variation) under s.58(4) may be made by or on behalf of:

- The child to whom the order or direction relates
- A person having parental rights over the child
- A relevant person
- Any person to whom notice of the application for the order was given by virtue of rules
- The applicant for the order made under s.57 [s.60(7)]

■ An application under s.60(7) must be made in relation to a CPO made under s.56, or a direction given under s.58, before the commencement of a children's hearing arranged in accordance with s.59(2) and in relation to such an order or direction continued (with or without variation) by virtue of s.59(4) 59, within 2 working days of such continuation, and any such application shall be determined within 3 working days of being made [s.60(8)]

Emergency Protection of Children when CPO Not Available [s.61]

Application & Conditions for s.61 Authorisation

■ On the application of any person, a justice of the peace (JP) may grant an authorisation under s.61 **if** s/he is satisfied:

- Both that the conditions laid down for the making of a CPO in s.57(1) are satisfied (is or will suffer significant harm) and that it is probable that any such order, if made, would contain an authorisation in terms of removal or prevention of a child's removal under s.57(4) **but that**
- It is not practicable in the circumstances for an application for such an order to be made to the sheriff or for the sheriff to consider such an application [s.61(1)]

■ On the application of a local authority a JP may grant an authorisation under s.61 **if** s/he is satisfied:

- Both that the conditions laid down for the making of a CPO in s.57(2) are satisfied (local authority enquiries being frustrated) and that it is probable that any such order, if made, would contain an authorisation in terms of removal or prevention of a child's removal under s.57(4) but that
- It is not practicable in the circumstances for an application for such an order to be made to the

sheriff or for the sheriff to consider such an application [s.61(2)]

Effect of Authorisation

■ An authorisation under s.61 may:

- Require any person in a position to do so to produce the child to the applicant
- Prevent any person from removing a child from a place where he is then being accommodated
- Authorise the applicant to remove the child to a place of safety and to keep him there until the expiration of the authorisation [s.61(3)]

Duration of Authorisation

■ An authorisation under s.61 ceases to have effect by **whichever is the earlier** of the following:

- 12 hours after the authorisation was made, if within that time, arrangements have not been made to prevent the child's removal from any place specified in the authorisation; or s/he has not been, or is not being, taken to a place of safety; or
- When such arrangements as above have been made or s/he has been so taken, when 24 hours have expired since it was so given; or an application for a CPO is disposed of [s.61(4)]

■ A police officer may remove the child to such a place and keep her/him there if s/he has reasonable cause to believe that:

- The conditions for the making of a CPO laid down in s.57(1) are satisfied
- It is not practicable in the circumstances for her/him to make an application for such an order to the sheriff or for the sheriff to consider such an application; and
- In order to protect the child from significant harm (or further such harm), it is necessary for her/him to remove the child to a place of safety [s.61(5)]

NB. S.61(5)) authorises the keeping of a child in a place of safety for a maximum of 24 hours from the time when the child is so removed and the authority to keep a child in a place of safety ceases on the disposal of an application in relation to the child for a CPO [s.61(6);(7)]

■ Where the Principal Reporter considers that the conditions for the grant of an authorisation under s.61 (1) or (2) above or the exercise of the power conferred by s.61 (5) above are not satisfied, or that it is no longer in the best interests of the child that s/he should be so kept:

- A child must not be kept in a place of safety or prevented from being removed from any place [s.61(8)]

Regulations in Respect of Emergency Child Protection Measures [s.62]

■ The Secretary of State has made regulations concerning the duties in respect of a child of any person removing her/him to, and keeping her/him in, a place of safety under s.61 above and they require:

- Notification of the removal of a child to be given to a person specified in the regulations
- Intimation to be given to any person of the place of safety at which a child is being kept
- Notification to be given to any person of the ceasing to have effect, under s.61 (4) of an authorisation [s.62].

Children Arrested by Police

Review of Case of Child Arrested by Police [s.63]

■ If the Principal Reporter has been informed by police in accordance with s.296 (3) Criminal Procedure (Scotland) Act 1975, that charges are not to be proceeded with against a child who has been detained in a place of safety, the Principal Reporter must, unless s/he considers compulsory measures of supervision are not required, arrange a children's hearing to which s/he must refer the case [s.63 (1)].

■ A children's hearing arranged under s.63 (1)) must begin not later than the 3rd day after the Principal Reporter received the information from the police [s.63 (2)].

- When the Principal Reporter considers a child of whose detention s/he has been informed does not require compulsory measures of supervision, s/he must direct that the child shall no longer be kept in the place of safety [s.63(3)].

- Subject to the above condition, a child who has been detained in a place of safety may continue to be kept at that place until the commencement of a children's hearing arranged under s.63(1) [s.63(4)].

- Subject to s.63(6) below, a children's hearing arranged under s.63(1) above may:

  - If it is satisfied the conditions mentioned in s.66(2) are satisfied, grant a warrant to keep the child in a place of safety and
  - Direct the Principal Reporter to arrange a children's hearing for the purposes of s.65(1)

  NB. S.66 (3) – (8) apply to a warrant granted under s.65 (5) as they apply to a warrant granted under s.66 (1) [s.63 (5)].

- A child must not be kept in a place of safety in accordance with a warrant granted under s.63(5) where the Principal Reporter, having regard to the welfare of the child, considers (as a result of a change in the circumstances of the case or of further information s/he receives) that:

  - The conditions mentioned in s.66(2) are no longer satisfied or the child is not in need of compulsory measures of supervision and

- When s/he does so consider must give notice to that effect to the person who is keeping the child in that place in accordance with the warrant [s.63(6)]

Business Meeting Preparatory to Children's Hearing

Business Meeting Preparatory to Children's Hearing [s.64]

■ At any time prior to the commencement of proceedings at a children's hearing, the Principal Reporter may arrange a 'business meeting' with members of the children's panel from which the children's hearing is to be constituted [s.64(1)]

■ When a business meeting is arranged, the Principal Reporter must give notice to the child in respect of whom the proceedings are to be commenced and any relevant person in relation to the child, of:

- The arrangement of the meeting and the matters which may be considered and determined by the meeting
- Their right to make their views on those matters known to the Principal Reporter and
- The duty of the Principal Reporter to present those views to the meeting [s.64(2)]

■ A business meeting, subject to s.64(4) below;

- Must determine such procedural and other matters as prescribed by Children's Hearing (Scotland) Rules SI 1996/3261
- May give such direction or guidance to the Principal Reporter in relation to the performance of her/his functions in relation to the proceedings as members think appropriate [s.64(3)]

■ Before a business meeting makes such a determination or gives such direction or guidance to the Principal Reporter, the Principal Reporter must present, and members must consider, any views expressed to her/him by the child or any relevant person [s.64(4)].

*NB. A business meeting is **not** a children's hearing so the rules applicable to hearings (other than those relating to publicity and appeals) do not apply.*

Referral to & Disposal of Case by Children's Hearing

Referral to & Proceedings at Children's Hearing [s.65]

■ The Principal Reporter is obliged to:

- Refer to the children's hearing, for consideration and determination on its merits, the case of any child in respect of whom s/he is satisfied that compulsory measures of supervision are necessary, and at least 1 of the grounds specified in s.52(2) of this Act is established and

- State such grounds in accordance with rules made under s. 42(1) i.e. Children's Hearing (Transmission of Information etc, (Scotland) Regulations 1996 (SI 1996/3260) and Children's Hearings (Scotland) Rules 1996 (SI 1996/3261) [s.65(1)]

■ When a referral is made in respect of a child who is subject to a s.57 CPO and that order is continued under s.59 or s.60, the Principal Reporter must arrange for the children's hearing under s.65 (1) above to take place on the 8th working day after the order was implemented [s.65 (2)].

■ When a referral is made in respect of a child who is already subject to a supervision requirement, the children's hearing must, before disposing of the referral, review that requirement in accordance with s.73 [s.65(3)].

■ Subject to s.65 (9) and (10) below, the chairperson of the children's hearing to whom a child's case has been referred must explain to the child and the relevant person, at the opening of proceedings on the referral, the grounds stated by the Principal Reporter for the referral so as to ascertain whether these grounds are accepted in whole or in part by them [s.65 (4)].

■ When the chairperson has given the explanation required by s.65 (3) above and the child and the relevant person **accept the grounds for the referral,** the children's hearing must proceed in accordance with s.69 [s.65(5)].

■ When the chairperson has given the explanation required by s.65 (3) above and the child and the relevant person **accept the grounds in part**, the children's hearing **may**, if members consider it appropriate to do so, proceed in accordance with s.69 with respect to those grounds which are accepted [s.65(6)].

■ When the chairperson has given the explanation required under s.65(3) above and either or both of the child and the relevant person **do not accept the grounds for the referral or accept the grounds in part, but the hearing's members do not consider it appropriate to proceed with the case**, the hearing must **either:**

- Direct the Principal Reporter to make an application to the sheriff for a finding as to whether such grounds for the referral as are not accepted by the child and the relevant person, are established **or**
- Must discharge the referral [s65(7)]

■ It is the duty of the chairperson to explain to the child and relevant person (assuming s/he is present) the purpose for which the application to the sheriff is being made and to inform the child s/he is under an obligation to attend the hearing before the sheriff [s.65 (8) ;(10)].

■ When a children's hearing is satisfied that the child for any reason will not be capable of understanding the explanation of the grounds for the referral required under s.65(3) or has not understood an explanation given under that subsection, members must either:

- Direct the Principal Reporter to make an application to the sheriff for a finding as to whether any referral grounds are established or
- Discharge the referral [s.65(9)]

Warrant to Keep Child if Children's Hearing Unable to Dispose of Case [s.66]

Conditions for Granting a Warrant

■ As well as any other power under Part 2 and subject to s.66 (5) below, a children's hearing arranged to consider a child's case under this Part and unable to dispose of the case:

- **May**, if satisfied that 1 of the conditions mentioned in s.66 (2) below is met, grant a warrant under s.66 (1)

■ The conditions referred to above are that:

- There is reason to believe that the child may not attend at any hearing of her/his case; or fail to comply with a requirement under s.69(3) or
- It is necessary that the child should be kept in a place of safety in order to safeguard or promote her/his his welfare [s.66(2)]

Effect of Warrant

■ A warrant under s.66(1) may require any person named in the warrant to:

- Find/keep the child in a place of safety for a period not exceeding 22 days after the warrant is granted
- Bring the child before a children's hearing at such times as may be specified in the warrant [s.66(3)]

■ The warrant may contain such conditions as appear to the children's hearing to be necessary or expedient, and without prejudice to that generality, may:

- Subject to s.90, require the child to submit to any medical or other examination or treatment; and
- Regulate the contact with the child of any specified person or class of persons [s.66(4)]

NB. S.90 makes it clear that in the case of a child who has the capacity by virtue of s.2(4) of the Age of Legal Capacity (Scotland) Act 1991 (capacity of child with sufficient understanding to consent to surgical, medical or dental procedure or treatment), her/his consent to the required medical or other examination/treatment is required.

■ Subject to s.66 (8), at any time prior to its expiry, a warrant granted under s.66 may, on an application to the children's hearing, on cause shown by the

Principal Reporter, be continued in force, (with or without variation of any conditions imposed by virtue of s.66 (4)), by the children's hearing for a maximum of 22 days as appears to them to be necessary [s.66 (5)].

■ When a children's hearing is satisfied that either of the criteria specified in s.70(10) are satisfied (risk of and from absconding and likelihood of injuring self or others), it may order that, pending disposal of the case, the child will be liable to be placed and kept in secure accommodation within a residential establishment at such times as the person in charge of that establishment, with the agreement of the chief social work officer of the relevant local authority, considers necessary [s.66(6)].

NB. When a children's hearing grants a warrant under s.66(1) or continue such a warrant under s.66(5), it may order that the place of safety at which the child is to be kept is not disclosed to any person or class of persons specified in the order [s.66(7)].

■ A child must **not** be kept in a place of safety or secure accommodation by virtue of s.66 for a period exceeding 66 days from the day s/he was first taken to a place of safety under a s.66(1) [s.66(8)].

Warrant for Further Detention of Child [s.67]

■ When a child is being kept in a place of safety by virtue of a warrant granted under s.66 or s.67(1), the

Principal Reporter at any time prior its expiry may apply to the sheriff for a warrant to keep the child in that place after either of those warrants has expired [s.67(1)].

■ A warrant under s.67(1) can only be granted on cause shown and:

- Must specify the date it will expire and
- May contain any such requirement or condition as may be contained in a s.66 warrant [s.67(2)]

■ When the sheriff grants a warrant under s.67(1) s/he may also make an order under s.67(3) in such terms as are mentioned in s.66(6) or (7) and any such order ceases to have effect when the warrant expires [s.67(3)].

■ An application under s.67(1) may be made at the same time as, or during the hearing of, an application which the Principal Reporter has been directed by a children's hearing to make under s.65(6) or (8) [s.67(4)].

Application to Sheriff to Establish Grounds of Referral [s.68]

■ S.68 applies to applications by the Reporter under s.65 (7) and s.67 (9).

NB. The former refers to a situation in which the grounds of referral explained to the child/relevant person have not been accepted; the latter to when the grounds have not been/will not be understood by the child and the hearing has not considered it appropriate to discharge the referral.

■ An application must be heard by the sheriff within 28 days of its being lodged [s.68 (2)].

■ When 1 of the grounds for the referral to which an application relates is the condition referred to in s.52(2)(i), i.e. the child has committed an offence:

- The application must be made to the sheriff who would have jurisdiction if the child were being prosecuted for that offence and
- In hearing the application in relation to that ground, the standard of proof required in criminal proceedings apply [s.68(3)]

■ A child has the right to attend the hearing of an application and (subject to s.68(5)), is under an obligation to attend such hearing

■ Though each has a right to be legally represented, the child and the relevant person may be represented by someone other than a legally qualified person at any date fixed by the sheriff for the hearing of the application [s.68 (4)].

■ The sheriff **may** dispense with the obligation imposed under s.68(4) for the child to attend where s/he is satisfied that:

- In an application in which the ground of referral to be established is one of the following conditions mentioned in s. 52(2) – (Sch. 1 offence/child is or is likely to become a member of the household of victim or perpetrator of Sch.1 offences/incest and intercourse with child by step-parent or person in position of trust condition) the obligation to attend of the child is not necessary for the just hearing of that application; **and**

- In any application, that it would be detrimental to the interests of the child for her/him to be present at the hearing of the application [s.68(5)]

■ If the child fails to attend the hearing of an application at which her/his obligation to attend has not been dispensed with, the sheriff may grant an order to find and keep the child and any such order provides authority for bringing the child before the sheriff and, (subject to s.68 (7) below), for keeping him in a place of safety until the sheriff can hear the application [s.68(6)].

NB. The child cannot be kept in a place of safety by virtue of s.68 (6) beyond the earlier of the expiry of 14 days beginning with the day on which s/he is found or disposal of the application by the sheriff [s.68(7)].

■ When in the course of the hearing of an application under s. 65(7), the child and the relevant person accept any of the grounds for referral to which the application relates, the sheriff must dispense with the hearing of evidence relating to that ground and deem the ground to be established for the purposes of the application (unless s/he is satisfied that, in all the circumstances of the case, the evidence should be heard).

■ When in the course of the hearing of an application under s. 65(9), the relevant person accept any of the grounds for referral to which the application relates, the sheriff may, it appears reasonable to her/him to do so, dispense with the hearing of evidence relating to that ground and deem the ground to be established for the purposes of the application (**unless** s/he is satisfied that, in all the circumstances of the case, the evidence should be heard) [s.68(8)].

■ When a sheriff decides that none of the grounds for referral in respect of which an application has been made are established, s/he is obliged to dismiss the application, discharge the referral to the children's hearing in respect of those grounds and recall, discharge or cancel any order, warrant, or direction relating to the protection and supervision of children [s.68(9)]

■ When the sheriff, after the hearing of any evidence or on acceptance in accordance with s.68 (8) above, finds that any of the grounds for the referral to which the application relates is, or should be deemed to be, established, s/he **must** remit the case to the Principal Reporter to make arrangements for a children's hearing to consider and determine the case.

■ The sheriff **may** also, if satisfied that keeping the child in a place of safety is necessary in her/his best interests **or** there is reason to believe s/he will run away before the children's hearing sit to consider the case, issue an order requiring (subject to s.68(12)) the child to be kept in a place of safety until that hearing [s.68(10)]

■ An order issued under s.68 (10) may, if the sheriff is satisfied that either of the criteria mentioned in s. 70(10) is fulfilled, provide that the child is liable to be placed and kept in secure accommodation within a residential establishment at such times as the person in charge of it, with the agreement of the chief social work officer of the relevant local authority, considers necessary [s.68 (11)].

NB. The s.70(10) criteria are that the child having previously absconded, is likely to abscond unless kept in secure accommodation and if s/he absconds, it is likely her/his physical/mental/moral welfare will be at risk or is likely to injure self/some other person unless kept in such accommodation.

■ A child must not be kept in a place of safety by virtue of s.68(10)(b) ('necessary in child's best interest' or 'is reason to believe s/he will run away before the hearing') after whichever is the earlier of the:

- Expiry of 3 days beginning with the day on which s/he is first so kept or
- Consideration of her/his case by the children's hearing arranged under s.68(10) above [s.68(12)]

Continuation or Disposal of Referral by Children's Hearing [s.69]

■ When the grounds of referral of the child's case stated by the Principal Reporter are accepted or established in accordance with s. 67 or s. 84, the children's hearing must consider those grounds, any report obtained under s.56(7) and any other relevant information available to them and must:

- Continue the case to a subsequent hearing in accordance with s.69(2) below
- Discharge the referral of the case in accordance with s.69(12) below or
- Make a supervision requirement under s.70 [s.69(1)]

■ The children's hearing may continue the case to a subsequent hearing where it is satisfied that, in order to complete its consideration of the case, it is necessary to have a further investigation [s.69(2)].

■ When a children's hearing continue the case under s.69(2), it may, for the purposes of that investigation, require the child to attend, or reside at, any clinic, hospital or other establishment during a period not exceeding 22 days [s.69(3)].

■ When a child fails to fulfil a requirement made under s.69(3), the children's hearing may, either on an application by the Principal Reporter or of its own motion, grant a warrant which provides the authority to:

- Find the child
- Remove her/him to a place of safety and keep her/him there and
- (Where the place of safety is not the clinic, hospital or other establishment referred to in the requirement made under s.69(3)) to take the child from the place of safety to such clinic, hospital or other establishment for the purposes of the investigation [s.69 (4);(5)]

■ A s.69 (4) warrant must be granted for such period as appears to the children's hearing to be appropriate, though cannot permit the keeping of a child in a place of safety after whichever is the earlier of the:

- Expiry of 22 days after the warrant is granted or
- Day on which the subsequent hearing of the child's case by a children's hearing begins [s.69(6)]

■ The children's hearing may grant a warrant requiring that the child be taken to and kept in a place of safety, where a child's case has been continued under s.69(2) and it is satisfied that:

- Keeping the child in a place of safety is necessary in the interests of safeguarding or promoting her/his welfare or
- There is reason to believe that the child may not attend the subsequent hearing of her/his case [s.69(7)]

- A s.69(7) warrant ceases to have effect on whichever is the earlier of the:

  - Expiry of 22 days after the warrant is granted; or
  - Day on which the subsequent hearing of the child's case by a children's hearing begins [s.69(8)]

- Warrants under s.69(4) or s.69(7) may contain such conditions as appear to the children's hearing to be necessary or expedient, and may (subject to s.90) require the child to submit to any medical or other examination or treatment and/or regulate the contact with the child of any specified person or class of persons [s.69(9)].

- If a child is to be kept at a place of safety under a s.69 warrant or is to attend, or reside at, any place in accordance with a requirement made under s.69 (3), the children's hearing may order that its location is not disclosed to any person or class of persons specified in the order [s.69(10)].

- If a child is to reside in a residential establishment by virtue of a requirement made or warrant granted under s.69, the children's hearing may, if satisfied that either of the criteria mentioned in section 70(10) is fulfilled, order that while the requirement or warrant remains in effect, s/he is liable to be placed in secure accommodation within that establishment at such times as the person in charge of the establishment, with the agreement of the chief social work officer of the relevant local authority, considers necessary [s.69(11)].

NB. The s.70(10) criteria are that the child having previously absconded, is likely to abscond unless kept in secure accommodation and if s/he absconds, it is likely her/his physical/mental/moral welfare will be at risk or is likely to injure self/some other person unless kept in such accommodation

- When a children's hearing decides not to make a supervision requirement under s.70 it is obliged to discharge the referral [s.69 (12)].

- On the discharge of the referral of the case, any order, direction, or warrant under children's hearings or protection and supervision provisions cease to have effect [s.69 (13)].

Disposal of Referral by Children's Hearing: Supervision Requirements, including Residence in Secure Accommodation [s.70]

- When the children's hearing to whom a child's case has been referred under s.65(1) is satisfied that compulsory measures of supervision are necessary in respect of the child it may make a 'supervision requirement' [s.70(1)]

- If the hearing decides to make such a supervision requirement, it must consider whether to impose any conditions with respect to contact between the child and any specified person/class of person as per s.70 (5) [s.70 (2)].

- A supervision requirement may require the child to:

- • Reside at any place or places specified in the requirement and
- • Comply with any condition contained in the requirement [s.70(3)]

■ The place/s specified in a s.70(3) requirement may be in England or Wales and a supervision requirement is authority for the person in charge of such a place to restrict the child's liberty to such extent as that person may consider appropriate, having regard to the terms of the requirement [s.70(4)].

■ A condition imposed under s.70 (3) above may:

- • Subject to s.90, require the child to submit to any medical or other examination or treatment
- • Regulate the contact with the child of any specified person or class of persons [s.70(5)]

■ A children's hearing may require, when making a supervision requirement, that any place where the child is to reside in accordance with the requirement is not disclosed to any person/class of persons specified [s.70(6)].

■ A children's hearing which makes a supervision requirement may determine that the requirement is reviewed at such time during the duration of the requirement as it determines [s.70 (7)].

■ A children's hearing may specify in the requirement that the child is liable to be placed and kept in secure accommodation in that establishment during such period as the person in charge of that establishment, with the agreement of the chief social work officer of the relevant local authority, considers necessary **if** it is satisfied that:

- It is necessary to make a supervision requirement which includes a requirement under s.70 (3) that the child reside in a named residential establishment and
- Any of the criteria specified in s.70 (10) are satisfied [s.70(9)]

NB. The criteria referred to in s.70(9) are that the child having previously absconded, is likely to abscond unless kept in secure accommodation, and, if s/he absconds, it is likely her/his physical/mental/moral welfare will be at risk or is likely to injure self/some other person unless kept in such accommodation [s.70(10)].

Duties of Local Authorities with Respect to Supervision Requirements [s.71]

- A supervision requirement must be given effect to by the local authority for whose area the children's hearing sits [s.71 (1)].

- When a supervision requirement provides that the child must reside in relevant accommodation or in any other accommodation not provided by a local authority, it:

  - Must from time to time investigate whether, while the child is so resident, any conditions

> imposed by the supervision requirement are
> being fulfilled
> • May take such steps as it considers reasonable if
>   it finds that such conditions are not being
>   fulfilled [s.71(2)]

*NB. 'Relevant accommodation' means
accommodation provided by parents or relatives of
the child or by any person associated with them or
with the child [s.71 (3)].*

Transfer of Child Subject to Supervision Requirement in Case of Necessity [s.72]

■ In any case of urgent necessity, where it is in the
interests of a child who is required by a supervision
requirement imposed under s.70 (3) to reside in a
specific residential establishment or specific other
accommodation **or** other children in that
establishment or accommodation, the chief social
work officer of the relevant local authority may direct
that (notwithstanding that requirement), the child
be transferred to another place [s.72 (1)].

■ Any child transferred under s.72 (1) must have
her/his case reviewed, in accordance with s.73 (8)
by a children's hearing within 7 days of transfer
[s.72 (2).

Duration & Review of Supervision Requirement [s.73]

■ No child is permitted to be subject to a supervision requirement for any period longer than is necessary in the interests of promoting or safeguarding her/his welfare [s.73(1)].

■ Subject to any variation or continuation of a supervision requirement under s.73 (9), no supervision requirement may remain in force for a period longer than 1 year [s.73 (2)].

■ A supervision requirement ceases to have effect when the young persons attains the age of 18 years [s.73 (3)].

■ A relevant local authority must refer the case of a child who is subject to a supervision requirement to the Principal Reporter where it is satisfied that:

- The requirement in respect of the child ought to cease to have effect or be varied
- A condition contained in the requirement is not being complied with or
- The best interests of the child would be served by it applying under s.86 for a parental responsibilities order; applying under s.18 of the Adoption (Scotland) Act 1978 for an order freeing the child for adoption or placing the child for adoption **and** it intends to apply for such an order or so place the child [s.73(4)]

- When the relevant local authority is aware that an application has been made and is pending; is about to be made, under s.12 of the Adoption (Scotland) Act 1978 for an adoption order in respect of a child who is subject to a supervision requirement, it must forthwith refer her/his case to the Principal Reporter [s.73(5)].

- A child or any relevant person may require a review of a supervision requirement in respect of the child at any time at least 3 months after the date:

  - On which the requirement is made; or
  - Of the most recent continuation, or variation, by virtue of s.73 of the requirement [s.73(6)]

- When a child is subject to a supervision requirement and (other than in accordance with that requirement or with an order under s.11), a relevant person proposes to take the child to live outside of Scotland, the person must, not later than 28 days before so taking the child, give notice of that proposal in writing to the Principal Reporter and to the relevant authority [s.73 (7)].

- The Principal Reporter must:

  - Arrange for a children's hearing to review any supervision requirement in respect of a child where the case has been referred to her/him under s.73(4) or (5); the review has been required under s.73(6); the review is required by virtue of s.70(7) or s.72(2); s/he has received in respect of the child such notice as is mentioned in s.73(7) **or** in any other case, the supervision requirement will expire within 3 months; and

■ The Principal Reporter must also make any arrangements incidental to that review [s.73 (8)].

■ When a supervision requirement is reviewed by a children's hearing arranged under s.73(8) above, it may:

- If satisfied that in order to complete the review of the supervision requirement it is necessary to have a further investigation of the child's case, continue the review to a subsequent hearing
- Terminate the requirement
- Vary the requirement
- Insert any requirement which could have been imposed by it under s.70(3) of or
- Continue the requirement, with or without such variation or insertion [s.73(9)]

NB. Having reviewed the case and where it decides further information is required, the hearing has similar powers to require the child to undergo investigative assessment or be kept in a place of safety as if it were a hearing which determined whether to impose a supervision requirement.

■ When a children's hearing vary or impose a requirement under s.73(9) which requires the child to reside in any specified place or places, it may order that such place or places must not be disclosed to any person or class of persons specified in the requirement [s.73(11)].

■ When a children's hearing is arranged under s.73 (8) on the grounds that the supervision requirement will expire within 3 months, it must consider whether (if the supervision requirement is not continued), the child still requires supervision or guidance

NB. When a children's hearing consider such supervision or guidance is necessary, it is the duty of the local authority to provide such supervision or guidance as the child is willing to accept [s.73 (12)].

■ Where a children's hearing is arranged by virtue of the 'best interests' provision of s.73 (4) or s.73 (5), then irrespective of what the hearing does under s.73 (9) it must draw up a report to provide advice for any court which may subsequently require to come to a decision, in relation to the child concerned, such as that mentioned in s.73 (14) in respect of the:

• Proposed application under s.86 (parental responsibility order) or under s.18 of the Adoption (Scotland) Act (freeing child for adoption), or

• Proposed placing for adoption or the application, or prospective application, under s.12 of the Adoption (Scotland) Act 1978 [s.73(13)]

NB. A court considering whether to grant an application under s.86 or under ss.18 or 12 of the Adoption (Scotland) Act 1978 and which, by virtue of s.73(13) must consider such a report before coming to a decision in the matter[s.73(14)].

Further Provision as Respects Children Subject to Supervision Requirements [s.74]

■ The Secretary of State may by regulations provide for:

- Transmission of information about a child subject to a supervision requirement to any person who, by virtue of that requirement, has, or is to have, control over her/him
- Temporary accommodation, where necessary, of such a child and
- Conveyance of such a child to any place in which, under the supervision requirement, s/he is to reside; to which s/he falls to be taken under of s.82(1) or s.82(5) or to any person to whom s/he falls to be returned s.82 (3)

Powers of Secretary of State with Respect to Secure Accommodation [s.75]

■ The Secretary of State has (Secure Accommodation (Scotland) Regulations 1996 (SI 1996/3255) made provision with respect to the placing in secure accommodation of any child who is:

- Subject to a requirement imposed under s.70(3) to reside at a specified place, but not subject to a requirement under s.70(9) or
- Not subject to a supervision requirement but who is being looked after by a local authority in pursuance of such enactments as may be specified in the regulations [s.75(1)]

- The above regulations:

  - Specify the circumstances in which a child may be so placed under the regulations
  - Make provision to enable a child who has been so placed or any relevant person to require that the child's case be brought before a children's hearing within a shorter period than would apply under regulations made under s.75(3) and
  - Specify different circumstances for different cases or classes of case [s.75(2)]

- Subject to s.75(4) and without prejudice to s.75(2)(b), the Secretary of State may prescribe the:

  - Maximum period during which a child may be kept in secure accommodation without the authority of a children's hearing or of the sheriff
  - Period within which a children's hearing must be arranged to consider the case of a child placed in secure accommodation by virtue of regulations made under s.75 (different periods may be so prescribed in respect of different cases or classes of case).

  NB. Regulations under s.75 impose a 66 day maximum for detention of a child in secure accommodation [s.75 (4)].

- The Secretary of State has by regulations varied the period within which a review of a condition imposed under s.70(9) must be reviewed under s.73 [s.75(5)]

■ The Secretary of State has by regulations made provision for the procedures to be applied in placing children in secure accommodation and these:

- Specify the duties of the Principal Reporter in relation to the placing of children in secure accommodation
- Made provision for the referral of cases to a children's hearing for review and
- Made provision for any person with parental responsibilities in relation to the child to be informed of the placing of the child in secure accommodation [s.75(6)]

Exclusion orders

Exclusion Orders [s.76]

■ Subject to s.76(3) to (9), where on the application of a local authority the sheriff is satisfied, in relation to a child, that the conditions mentioned in s.76(2) below are met, s/he may grant an 'Exclusion Order') excluding from the child's family home 'the named person' [s.76(1)].

Conditions for Obtaining an Exclusion Order

■ The conditions are that the:

- Child has suffered, is suffering, or is likely to suffer, significant harm as a result of any conduct, or any threatened or reasonably apprehended conduct, of the named person

- Making of an Exclusion Order against the named person is necessary for the protection of the child (irrespective of whether the child is for the time being residing in the family home) **and** would better safeguard the child's welfare than the removal of the child from the family home; **and**
- If an order is made, there will be an 'appropriate person' specified in the application capable of taking responsibility for the provision of appropriate care for the child and any other member of the family who requires it and who is, or will be, residing in the family home

■ No application under s.76(1) for an Exclusion Order shall be finally determined unless the:

- Named person has been afforded an opportunity of being heard by, or represented before, the sheriff and the
- Sheriff has considered any views expressed by any person on whom notice of the application has been served in accordance with rules making such provision under s.91 [s.76(3)]

■ On an application under s.76(1) the sheriff may grant an interim order, which will have effect as an Exclusion Order pending a hearing by the sheriff under s.76 (5) held within such period as may be specified in **if:**

- S/he is satisfied in accordance with s.76(1) but
- The named person has not has an opportunity of being heard or represented; or the sheriff has

not considered any views expressed by persons on whom notice has been served as per s.73(3) [s.76(4)]

- The sheriff must conduct a hearing under s.76 (5) within such period as specified Act of Sederunt (Family Proceedings in the Sheriff Court) (SI 1996/2167) made by virtue of s.91 and, if satisfied at that hearing as per s.76 (1) above, may before finally determining the application, confirm or vary the interim order, or any term or condition on which it was granted, or may recall such an order [s.76 (5)].

- When the conditions of s.76 (3) have been fulfilled, the sheriff may, at any point prior to the final determination of the application, grant an interim order [s.76 (6)].

  NB. An order under s.76 (5) or (6) above has effect as an Exclusion Order pending the final determination of the application [s.76 (7)].

- When an application is made under s.76(1) above and the sheriff considers the conditions for making a Child Protection Order under s.57 are satisfied, s/he may make an such an order as if the application had been duly made by the local authority under s.57 rather than s.76 [s.76(8)].

- The sheriff must not make an Exclusion Order if it appears to her/him that to do so would be unjustifiable or unreasonable, having regard to:

  - All the circumstances of the case, including 'matters' specified in s.76(10) below; and

- Any 'requirement' such as is specified in s.76(11) below and the likely consequences in the light of that requirement of the exclusion of the named person from the family home [s.76(9)]

■ The 'matters' referred to in s.76(9) are the:

  - Conduct of the members of the child's family (in relation to each other or otherwise)
  - Respective needs and financial resources of the members of that family
  - Extent (if any) to which the family home and any relevant item in it is used in connection with a trade, business or profession by any member of the family [s.76(10)]

■ The 'requirement' referred to in s.76(9) above is a requirement that the named person (alone or with any other person) must reside in the family home, where that home:

  - Is or is part of an agricultural holding within the meaning of the Agricultural Holdings (Consequential Amendments) (Scotland) Order 2003 Sch.1 para.12 or
  - Is let, or is a home in respect of which possession is given, to the named person (alone or with any other person) by an employer as an incident of employment [s.76(11)]

Effect of, & Orders etc. Ancillary to Exclusion Orders [s.77]

■ An Exclusion Order in respect of the home to which it relates, has the effect of suspending the named person's rights of occupancy (if any) and prevents her/him from entering the home, except with the express permission of the local authority which applied for the order [s.77(1)].

■ The sheriff, on the application of the local authority, may (if and in so far as s/he thinks fit, when making an Exclusion Order) do any of the things mentioned in s.77 (3) below.

■ The sheriff is empowered to grant:

- A warrant for the summary ejection of the named person from the home
- An interdict prohibiting the named person from entering the home without the express permission of the local authority
- An interdict prohibiting the removal by the named person of any relevant item specified in the interdict from the home, except either with the written consent of the local authority, or of an appropriate person; or by virtue of a subsequent order of the sheriff
- An interdict prohibiting the named person from entering or remaining in a specified area in the vicinity of the home
- An interdict prohibiting the taking by the named person of any step of a kind specified in the interdict in relation to the child

- An order regulating the contact between the child and the named person

■ The sheriff may also make any other order which s/he considers necessary for the proper enforcement of a remedy granted by any of the first 3 bullet points above [s.77(3)]

■ No warrant, interdict or order (except one under s.77 (3) prohibiting the named person from entering the home without express permission of the local authority) may be granted or made under s.77 (2) if the named person satisfies the sheriff that it is unnecessary to do so [s.77 (4)].

■ When the sheriff grants a warrant of summary ejection under s.77(2) above in the absence of the named person, s/he may give directions as to the preservation of any of that person's goods and effects which remain in the family home [s.77(5)].

■ The sheriff may make an order regulating contact between the child and the named person irrespective of whether there has been an application for such an order [s.77(6)].

■ On the application of either the named person or the local authority, the sheriff may make the Exclusion Order, or any remedy granted under s.77(2) above, subject to such terms and conditions as s/he considers appropriate [s.77(7)].

Powers of Arrest etc. in Relation to Exclusion Order [s.78]

■ The sheriff may, whether or not on an application under s.78(2) below, attach a power of arrest to any interdict granted under s.77(2) by virtue of s.77 (3) [s.78(1)].

■ A local authority may at any time while an Exclusion Order has effect, apply for such attachment of a power of arrest [s.78(2)].

■ A power of arrest attached to an interdict by virtue of s.78 (1) above does not have effect until such interdict, together with the attached power of arrest, is served on the named person [s.78(3)].

■ If, by virtue of s.78(1) above, a power of arrest is attached to an interdict, the local authority must, as soon as possible after the interdict and the attached power of arrest, is served on the named person, ensure that documents (specified below) are delivered to:

- The chief constable of the police area in which the family home is situated; and
- (When the interdict was granted by virtue of s.77(3)(e)) the chief constable of the area in which the step or conduct which is prevented by the interdict may take place

■ The specified documents are a copy of the application for the interdict and of the interlocutor granting the interdict, together with a certificate of service of the interdict and, where the application to attach the power of arrest was made after the interdict was granted, a copy of that application and of the interlocutor above granting it and a certificate of service of the interdict together with the attached power of arrest [s.78 (4)].

- When any interdict to which a power of arrest is attached by virtue of s.78 (1) is varied or recalled, the person who applied for the variation or recall must ensure there is delivered to each chief constable specified in s.78 (4) a copy of the application for such variation or recall and of the interlocutor granting the variation or recall [s.78 (5)].

- A constable may arrest without warrant the named person if s/he has reasonable cause for suspecting that person to be in breach of an interdict to which a power of arrest has been attached by virtue of s.78(1) [s.78(6)].

- When a person has been arrested under s.78(6), the constable in charge of a police station may:

  - If satisfied there is no likelihood of that person further breaching the interdict to which the power of arrest was attached under s.78(1), liberate her/him unconditionally or
  - Refuse to liberate that person [s.78(7)]

- Such a refusal to liberate an arrested person and her/his detention until appearance in court by virtue of either s.78 (11) or any provision of the

Criminal Procedure (Scotland) Act 1975 as amended, cannot subject that constable to any claim whatsoever [s.78(8)].

- When a person has been liberated under s.78 (7), the facts and circumstances which gave rise to the arrest must be reported to the procurator fiscal forthwith [s.78 (9)].

- S.78(11) to (13) below apply only where the:

  - Arrested person has not been released under s.78(7) and the
  - Procurator fiscal decides no criminal proceedings are to be taken in respect of the facts and circumstances which gave rise to the arrest [s.78(10)]

- A person arrested under s.78(6) must wherever practicable, be brought before the sheriff sitting as a court of summary criminal jurisdiction for the district in which s/he was arrested not later than in the course of the first day after the arrest

  NB. For the above purpose, a 'day' excludes Saturday, Sunday or a court holiday prescribed for that court under s.10 of the Bail etc. (Scotland) Act 1980, on which the sheriff is not sitting for the disposal of criminal business [s.78(11)].

- S.3(1) and s.3(3) Criminal Justice (Scotland) Act 1980 as amended (intimation to a person named by the person arrested) apply to a person arrested under s.78(6) above as they apply to a person who has been arrested in respect of an offence [s.78(12)].

■ When a person is pursuant to s.78(13) brought before the sheriff under s.78 (11) above, the procurator fiscal must present to the court a petition containing a:

- Statement of the particulars of the person arrested under s.78(6) above
- Statement of the facts and circumstances which gave rise to that arrest and
- Request that the person be detained for a further period not exceeding 2 days

■ The sheriff may order the arrested person to be detained for a period not exceeding 2 days if it appears to her/him that:

- The statement of the facts and circumstances which gave rise to the arrest above discloses a prima facie breach of interdict by the arrested person
- Proceedings for breach of interdict will be taken; and
- There is a substantial risk of violence by the arrested person against any member of the family, or an appropriate person, resident in the family home

■ The sheriff must in any case in which the above 3 bullet points do not apply, order the release of the arrested person from custody (unless s/he is in custody in respect of some other matter) [s.78(13)]

NB. In computing the period of 2 days referred to above, no account is to be taken of a Saturday, a

Sunday or any holiday in the court in which
proceedings for breach of interdict will require to be
raise [s.78(13)(b)].

■ When a person is liberated or is to be brought before
the sheriff the procurator fiscal must at the earliest
opportunity take all reasonable steps to intimate to
the local authority which made the application for
the interdict, an appropriate person who will reside
in, or who remains in residence in, the family home
mentioned in the order and any solicitor who acted
for the appropriate person when the interdict was
granted or to any other solicitor who the procurator
fiscal has reason to believe acts for the time being
for that person that:

• S/he has decided that no criminal proceedings
should be taken in respect of the facts and
circumstances which gave rise to the arrest of
the named person [s.78(14)]

Duration, Variation & Recall of Exclusion Order [s.79]

■ Subject to s.79(2) below, an Exclusion Order ceases
to have effect on a date 6 months after being made
[s.79(1)]

■ An exclusion order ceases to have effect on a date
prior to the 6 months cited above when:

• The order contains a direction by the sheriff that
it shall cease to have effect on that prior date

- The sheriff, on an application under s.79(3) recalls the order before the date so mentioned or
- Any permission given by a 3rd party to the spouse or partner of the named person, or to an appropriate person, to occupy the home to which the order relates is withdrawn [s.79(2)]

■ The sheriff may, on the application of the local authority, the named person, an appropriate person or the spouse or partner of the named person (if that spouse or partner is not excluded from the family home and is not an appropriate person), vary or recall an exclusion order and any warrant, interdict, order or direction granted or made under s.77 [s.79 (3)].

NB. For the purposes of s.79, partners are persons who live together in a family home as if they were husband and wife [s.79 (4)].

Exclusion Orders: Supplementary Provisions [s.80]

■ The Secretary of State may make regulations with respect to the powers, duties and functions of local authorities in relation to Exclusion Orders [s.80(1)] (see Act of Sederunt (Child Care Maintenance and Rules) (SI 1997/291).

■ An application for an Exclusion Order, or under s.78(3) for the variation or recall of such an order or of any thing done under s.76(2) must be made to the sheriff for the sheriffdom within which the family home is situated [s.80(2)].

Offences in Connection with Orders etc. for Protection of Children

Offences in Connection with Orders etc. for Protection of Children [s.81]

- A person shall (subject to s.38(3) and (4)) be guilty of an offence and liable on summary conviction to a fine not exceeding level 3 on the standard scale if s/he intentionally obstructs:

  - Any person acting under a Child Protection Order
  - Any person acting under an authorisation granted under s.61(1) or (2) or
  - A constable acting under s.61(5) [s.81(1)]

Fugitive Children & Harbouring

Recovery of Certain Fugitive Children [s.82]

- A child who absconds from a place of safety in which s/he is being kept, from a 'relevant place' other than a place of safety that is a residential establishment in which s/he is required to reside by virtue of s.70(3) or a hospital or other institution in which s/he is temporarily residing while subject to such a requirement or from a person who, by virtue of a supervision requirement or of s.74, has control over her/him while s/he is being taken to, is awaiting being taken to, or (whether or not by reason of being on leave) is temporarily away from, such place of safety or relevant place:

- May be arrested without warrant in any part of the UK and taken to the place of safety/relevant place; and a court which is satisfied there are reasonable grounds for believing that the child is within any premises may, where there is such power of arrest, grant a warrant authorising a constable to enter those premises and search for the child using reasonable force if necessary [s.82(1)]

■ Without prejudice to the generality of s.82 (1), a child who at the end of a period of leave from a place of safety/relevant place, fails to return there shall, for the purposes of this section be taken to have absconded [s.82 (2)]

NB. The same provisions apply to a child who absconds from the control of a person who has that control by virtue of a supervision requirement e.g. a foster carer but not a person who anyway has parental responsibilities or rights over the child [s.82(3)].

■ If a child is taken under s.82 (1) to a place of safety or relevant place or is returned under s.82 (3) to a person but the occupier of that place of safety/relevant place, or as the case may be that person, is unwilling or unable to receive her/him, that circumstance must be intimated forthwith to the Principal Reporter [s.82(4)].

■ When intimation is required by s.82 (4) the child must be kept in a place of safety until:

- In a case where s/he is subject to a supervision requirement, s/he can be brought before a children's hearing for that requirement to be reviewed or

- In any other case, the Principal Reporter has, in accordance with s.56(6) considered whether compulsory measures of supervision are required in respect of the child [s.82(5)]

Harbouring [s.83]

■ Subject to s.38(3) and (4) of this Act, to s.52(5) and (6) of the Children Act 1989 (applicable to England and Wales) and to Article 70(5) and (6) of the Children (Northern Ireland) Order 1995 a person is guilty of an offence and liable on summary conviction to a fine not exceeding level 5 on the standard scale or imprisonment for a term not exceeding 6 months or to both if s/he:

- Knowingly assists or induces a child to abscond in circumstances which render the child liable to arrest under s.82(1) or (3)

- Knowingly and persistently attempts to induce a child so to abscond

- Knowingly harbours or conceals a child who has so absconded

- Knowingly prevents a child from returning to a place of safety/relevant place as specified in s.82(1) or to a person who has control over the child by virtue of a s.74 or other supervision requirement [s.83(1)]

Implementation of Authorisations etc.

Implementation of Authorisations etc [s.84]

■ When an order, authorisation or warrant under s.39 to s.85 grants power to find a child and to keep her/him in a place of safety, such order/authorisation/warrant may be implemented as if it were a warrant for the apprehension of an accused person issued by a court of summary jurisdiction; and any enactment or rule of law applying to such a warrant can, subject to the provisions of this Act, apply [s.84]

New evidence: Review of Establishment of Grounds of Referral

Application for Review of Establishment of Grounds of Referral [s.85]

■ Subject to s.85(3) and (4) summarised below, an application may be made to the sheriff for a review of a s.68(10) finding (remittal for a children's hearing or detention in a place of safety) [s.85(1) &(2)].

■ An application under s.85(1) above may **only** be made when the applicant claims:

• To have evidence which was not considered by the sheriff on the original application which might materially have affected the determination of the original application

• That such evidence is likely to be credible and reliable and would have been admissible in relation to the ground of referral which was found to be established on the original application and

- That there is a reasonable explanation for the failure to lead such evidence on the original application [s.85(3)]

■ An application under s.85(1) above may only be made by:

- The child in respect of whom the ground of referral was found to be established or
- A 'relevant person' in relation to her/him

■ If the sheriff is **not** satisfied that any of the claims made in the application are established s/he is obliged to dismiss the application [s.85 (5)].

■ If the sheriff **is** satisfied that the claims made in the application are established, s/he must consider the evidence and if satisfied that **none** of the grounds of referral in the original application to which the application relates is established, must:

- Allow the application
- Discharge the referral to the children's hearing in respect of those grounds and
- Proceed in accordance with s.85 (7) below in relation to any supervision requirement about the child (whether or not varied under s.73) in so far as it relates to any such ground

■ If satisfied that any ground of referral in the original application **is** established, the sheriff may proceed in accordance with s.68 (10) [s.85 (6)].

- Where the sheriff is satisfied none of the grounds of the original application is satisfied s/he may:

  - Order any supervision requirement so mentioned to terminate immediately or on a date s/he will specify or
  - If satisfied there is evidence sufficient to establish any ground of referral (not stated in the original application) the sheriff may find such ground established and proceed in accordance with s.68(10) in relation to that ground [s.85(7)]

- When the sheriff specifies a date for the termination of a supervision requirement s/he may, before the termination, order a variation of that or any requirement imposed under s.70(6) of or of any determination made under s.70 (7), and such variation may take effect:

  - Immediately; or
  - On such date as s/he may specify [s.85(8)]

- When the sheriff orders the termination of a supervision requirement in accordance with s.85(7) s/he must consider whether, after such termination, the child concerned will still require supervision/guidance; and if s/he considers such supervision/guidance will be necessary must direct a local authority to provide it in accordance with s.85(10) below [s.85(9)].

- When a sheriff has given a direction under s.85(9) above, it is the duty of the local authority to comply

with that direction, though that duty is discharged
where it offers such supervision/guidance to the
child and (if of sufficient age and maturity to
understand what is being offered), is unwilling to
accept it [s.85(10)].

Parental Responsibilities Orders Etc

Parental Responsibilities Orders

Parental Responsibilities Order: General [s.86]

■ On the application of a local authority the sheriff may make a 'Parental Responsibilities Order' transferring to the local authority (only for such period as the order remains in force) the appropriate parental rights and responsibilities relating to a child [s.86 (1)].

■ A Parental Responsibilities Order can only be made if the sheriff is satisfied that each relevant person freely, and with full understanding of what is involved, agrees unconditionally that the order be made.

■ A Parental Responsibilities Order can also be made if the sheriff is satisfied that each 'relevant person' is a person who:

- Is not known, cannot be found or is incapable of giving agreement
- Is withholding such agreement unreasonably
- Has persistently failed, without reasonable cause, to fulfil one or other of the following parental responsibilities in relation to the child (responsibility to safeguard and promote the child's health, development and welfare or, if the child is not living with her/him, responsibility to maintain personal relations and direct contact with the child on a regular basis) or

- Has seriously ill-treated the child, whose reintegration into the same household as that person is, because of the serious ill-treatment or for other reasons, unlikely [s.86(2)]

NB. Reference to appropriate parental rights and responsibilities relating to the child is to all parental rights and responsibilities except any right to agree, or decline to agree to the placing of a child with parental consent, giving parental responsibility prior to adoption abroad, making of an application for 'freeing' or adoption abroad under English, Scottish or Northern Ireland legislation or to adoption itself [s.86(3)].

■ A person is a 'relevant person' for the purposes of s.86 if s/he is a parent of the child or a person who for the time being has parental rights in relation to her/him [s.86 (4)].

■ The sheriff may, in an order under s.86 impose such conditions as s/he considers appropriate; and may vary or discharge such an order on the application of:

- The local authority
- Child
- Any person who immediately before the making of the order is a relevant person or of any other person claiming an interest [s.86(5)]

■ An order under s.86 will, if not first discharged by the sheriff, terminate on the occurrence of any of the following:

- The child attains the age of 18 years
- The child is adopted
- An adoption agency is authorised to place her/him for adoption with parental consent
- The child becomes subject of a Placement Order or an order awarding parental responsibility prior to adoption abroad
- An order is made for the child's return under Part 1 Child Abduction and Custody Act 1985 or
- A decision (other than a decision relating to rights of access in s.25(2) of the above Act, is registered under s.16 of the same Act [s.86(6)]

Further Provision as Respects Parental Responsibilities Orders: General [s.87]

■ Subject to s.87 (2) and (3) below, where a Parental Responsibilities Order is made it is the duty of the local authority which applied for it (the 'appropriate authority') to fulfil the transferred responsibilities while the order remains in force [s.87(1)].

■ The appropriate authority **may** allow, for a fixed period or until it determines otherwise to allow the child to reside with her/his parent, guardian, relative or friend in any case where it appears to the authority that to allow this would be for the benefit of the child [s.87(2)].

■ When by virtue of s.87 (2) a child is residing with a person, the appropriate authority may by notice in writing to that person require her/him to return the child to the local authority by a time specified in the notice. Service of such notice must be effected either by the authority leaving it in the person's hands or by sending it to her/him, at her/his and the child's most recent known address, by recorded delivery service [s.87(3)].

■ For the purposes of any application for a Parental Responsibilities Order, rules prescribe:

- The person to act as 'curator ad litem' to the child in question at the hearing of the application, safeguarding her/his in such manner as may be so prescribed; and
- The person known as a 'reporting officer' to witness agreements to Parental Responsibilities Orders and to perform such other duties as may be so prescribed,

NB. One person maybe appointed to fulfil both the above roles but where the applicant is a local authority, no employee of it can be appointed [s.87(4)]

Parental Contact [s.88]

■ S.88 applies where a Parental Responsibilities Order is being made, or is in force [s.88 (1)].

■ The child must, subject to s.88 (3) below, be allowed reasonable contact by the appropriate authority with:

- Each person who, immediately before the making of the parental responsibilities order, is a 'relevant person' for the purposes of s.86

- • Where, immediately before that order was made a Residence or Contact Order was in force with respect to the child, the person in whose favour the relevant order made **or** a person was entitled to have the child residing with her/him under an order by a court of competent jurisdiction, that person [s.88(2)]

- ■ On an application made to her/him by the child, by the appropriate authority or by any person with an interest, the sheriff may make such order as s/he considers appropriate as to contact (if any) to be allowed between the child and any person specified in the order (whether or not one of those described in s.88 (2)) [s.88(3)].

- ■ A sheriff, on making a Parental Responsibilities Order, or at any time while such an order remains in force as may make an order under s.88(3) above as respects the child even where no application has been made in that regard [s.88(4)].

- ■ An order under s.88 may impose such conditions as the sheriff considers appropriate and s/he may vary or discharge such an order on the application of the child, the appropriate authority or any person with an interest [s.88(5)].

- ■ An order under s.88 must, if not first discharged by the sheriff, terminate when the Parental Responsibilities Order to which it is referable does [s.88 (6)].

Offences in Relation to Parental Responsibilities Orders [s.89]

- A person is guilty of an offence and liable, on summary conviction, to a fine not exceeding level 5 on the standard scale or to imprisonment for a term not exceeding 6 months or to both if s/he knowingly and without lawful authority or reasonable excuse:

  - Fails to comply with a notice under s.87(3)
  - Harbours or conceals a child as respects whom a Parental Responsibilities Order has been made and who has run away, or been taken away or whose return is required by such a notice, or
  - Induces, assists or incites a child as respects whom any such order has been made to run away, or stay away, from a place where s/he is looked after or who takes away such a child from that place [s.89].

Miscellaneous

Consent of Child to Certain Procedures [s.90]

- Nothing in Part II of the Act prejudices any capacity of a child enjoyed by virtue of s.2(4) Age of Legal Capacity (Scotland) Act 1991 (capacity of child with sufficient understanding to consent to surgical, medical or dental procedure or treatment).

- Hence, where s.66(4)(a), s.67(2) or s.69(9)(a) in a warrant; or s.70(5)(a) of this Act, in a supervision requirement requires a child to submit to any examination or treatment but s/he has the capacity mentioned above, the examination or treatment must only be carried out if the child consents [s.90].

NB. Though capacity to consent includes a capacity to refuse medical treatment, the above provision does not prevent a children's hearing from imposing a such a condition on a capable child.

Appendix 1: Convention Rights and Fundamental Freedoms [Articles 2–12 and 14 of Convention, Articles 1–3 First Protocol and Articles 1 and 2 Sixth Protocol, as read with Articles 16–18 of Convention]

With effect from 01.07.99, all courts in Scotland have been required, so far as is possible to interpret all legislation, whenever enacted, in a way which is compatible with the European Convention on Human Rights.

It is unlawful for public authorities to act in a way which is incompatible with Convention rights summarised in the following pages.

When introducing legislation, government must make a statement about the compatibility of the Bill with Convention rights.

Articles 2–12 & 14

Article 2 – Right to Life

Everyone's right to life shall be protected by law and no one shall be deprived of her/his life intentionally except in the execution of a sentence of a court following her/his conviction of a crime for which this penalty is provided in law.

This Article is not contravened if force, no more than absolutely necessary is used:

a) In defence of any person from unlawful violence

b) In order to effect a lawful arrest or to prevent the escape of a person lawfully detained

c) In action lawfully taken for the purpose of quelling a riot or insurrection

Relevant cases: Osman v UK [1999] 1 FLR 193, Keenan v UK (21 May 2001) EHRR 2001.

Article 3 – Prohibition of Torture

No one shall be subjected to torture or to inhuman or degrading treatment or punishment.

Relevant cases: A v UK [1998] 2 FLR 959; Z v UK [2001] 2FLR 612

Article 4 – Prohibition of Slavery and Forced Labour

No one shall be held in slavery or servitude.

No one shall be required to perform forced or compulsory labour.

Forced' or 'compulsory' labour excludes work required in the ordinary course of detention in accordance with Article 5 [see below] or during conditional release from such detention; any military service or its equivalent for conscientious objectors; any service exacted in the case of an emergency or calamity which threatens life or well being of the community; any work or service which forms part of normal civic obligations.

Article 5 – Right to Liberty & Security

1. Everyone has the right to liberty and security of person. No one shall be deprived of liberty except in the following cases and in accordance with a procedure described in law:

a) Lawful detention of a person after conviction by a competent court.

b) Lawful arrest or detention of a person for non-compliance with the lawful order of a court or in order to secure the fulfilment of any obligation prescribed below.

c) Lawful arrest or detention to bring a person before the competent legal authority on reasonable suspicion of having committed an offence (or when it is reasonably considered necessary to prevent her/him committing an offence or from fleeing having done so).

d) Detention of a minor by lawful order for purpose of educational supervision or lawful detention so as to bring her/him before the competent legal authority.

e) Lawful detention of persons for the prevention of the spreading of infectious diseases, of persons of unsound mind, alcoholics, drug addicts or vagrants.

f) Lawful arrest or detention of a person to prevent her/him effecting an unauthorised entry into the country or of a person against whom action is being taken with a view to deportation or extradition.

2. Everyone who is arrested must be informed promptly in a language s/he understands of the reasons and of any charges against them.

3. Everyone arrested/detained in accordance with para.1.c). above, must be brought promptly before a judge or another officer authorised by law to exercise judicial power and is entitled to trial within a reasonable period of time, or release pending trial or release may be conditioned by guarantees to appear for trial.

4. Everyone who is deprived of liberty by arrest/detention is entitled to take proceedings by which the lawfulness of her/his detention is decided speedily by a court and release ordered if the detention is not lawful.

5. Everyone who has been the victim of arrest/detention in contravention of the provisions of this Article has an enforceable right to compensation.

Article 6 – Right to Fair Trial

1. In the determination of her/his civil rights and obligations or of any criminal charge against them, everyone is entitled to a fair and public hearing within a reasonable time by an independent and impartial tribunal established by law. Judgement must be given publicly but the press and public may be excluded from all or part of the trial in the interests of morals, public order or national security in a democratic society; where

the interests of juveniles or the protection of the private life of the parties require it; or to the extent strictly necessary in the court's opinion in special circumstances where publicity would prejudice the interests of justice.

2. Everyone charged with a criminal offence must be presumed innocent until proved guilty according to law.

3. Everyone charged with a criminal offence has the following minimum rights:

a) To be informed promptly in a language s/he understands in detail of the nature and reason for the accusation.

b) To have adequate time and facilities for preparation of defence.

c) To defend her/himself in person or through legal assistance of the person's choosing, or if of insufficient means to pay for legal assistance to be given it free when the interests of justice require it.

d) To examine or have examined witnesses against her/him and to obtain the attendance and examination of witnesses on her/his behalf under the same conditions as witnesses against her/him.

e) To have the free assistance of an interpreter if s/he cannot understand or speak the language used in court.

Relevant cases: McMichael v UK 20 EHRR 205; H v UK 10 EHRR 95; Re: PC & S v UK [20002] 2 FLR 631.

Article 7 - No Punishment without Law

1. No one must be held guilty of any criminal offence on account of any act or omission which did not constitute a criminal offence under national or international law at the time when it was committed. Nor must a heavier penalty be imposed than the one which was applicable at the time the criminal offence was committed.

2. This Article must not prejudice the trial and punishment of any person for any act or omission which at the time it was committed was criminal according to the general principles of law recognised by civilised nations.

Article 8 - Right to Respect for Private & Family Life

1. Everyone has the right to respect for her/his private and family life, home and correspondence.

2. There must be no interference by a public authority with the exercise of this right except such as is in accordance with the law and is necessary in a democratic society in the interests of national security, public safety or the economic well being of the country, for the prevention of disorder or crime, for the protection of health or morals, or for the protection of the rights and freedoms of others.

Relevant cases: Yousef v Netherlands [2003] 1 FLR 210; Niemitz v Germany 16 EHRR 97; Botta v Holby 26 EHRR 241; Re: PC & S v UK [20002] 2 FLR 631.

Article 9 – Freedom of Thought, Conscience & Religion

1. Everyone has the right to freedom of thought, conscience and religion; this freedom includes freedom to change religion or belief and freedom either alone or in community with others and in public or in private, to manifest her/his religion or belief in worship, teaching, practice and observance.

2. Freedom to manifest one's religion or beliefs shall be subject to such limitations as are prescribed by law and are necessary in a democratic society in the interests of public safety, for the protection of public order, health or morals, or for the protection of the rights and freedoms of others.

Relevant case: Re J (Muslim Circumcision Specific Issue Order) [2000] 1 FLR 571.

Article 10 – Freedom of Expression

1. Everyone has the right of freedom of expression. This right shall include freedom to hold opinions and to receive and impart information and ideas without interference by public authority and regardless of frontiers. This Article shall not prevent States from requiring the licensing of broadcasting, television or cinema enterprises.

2.The exercise of these freedoms, since it carries with it duties and responsibilities may be subject to such formalities, conditions, restrictions or penalties as are prescribed by law and are necessary in a democratic society in the interest of national security, territorial integrity or public safety, for the protection of disorder or crime, for the protection of health or morals, for the protection of the reputation or rights of others, for preventing the disclosure of information received in confidence or for maintaining the authority and impartiality of the judiciary.

Article 11 - Freedom of Assembly & Association

1. Everyone has the right to freedom of peaceful assembly and to freedom of association with others including the right to form and join trades unions for the protection of her/his interests.

2. No restrictions shall be placed on the exercise of these rights other than such as are prescribed by law an are necessary in a democratic society in the interests of national security or public safety, for the prevention of disorder or crime or for the protection of the rights and freedoms of others. This Article shall not prevent the imposition of lawful restrictions on the exercise of these rights by members of the armed forces, of the police or of the administration of the State.

Article 12 - Right to Marry

Men and women of marriageable age have the right to marry and to found a family according to the national laws governing the exercise of that right.

Article 14 - Prohibition of Discrimination

The enjoyment of the rights and freedoms set forth in this Convention shall be secured without discrimination on any ground such as sex, race, colour, language, religion, political or other opinion, national or social origin, association with a national minority, property, birth or other status.

Breach of Article 14 cannot be argued on its own but must be linked with some other breach of a Convention Article e.g. Breach of Right To A Fair Trial' such as an argument that denying children rights to representation in residence and contact proceedings is based on discrimination on the grounds of age (Articles 6 and 14.)

Articles 1–3 First Protocol

Article 1 - Protection of Property

Every natural or legal person is entitled to the peaceful enjoyment of their possessions. No one shall be deprived of their possessions except in the public interest and subject to conditions provided for by law and the general principles of international law (this does not impair the right of the State to enforce necessary laws on use of property or to secure payment of taxes or other contributions or penalties).

Article 2 - Right to Education

No person shall be denied the right to education. In the exercise of any functions which it assumes in relation to education and teaching, the State shall respect the rights of parents to ensure such education and teaching in conformity with their own religious and philosophical convictions.

Relevant case: Campbell & Cosans v UK [1982] Series A, No.48 4 EHRR 293

Article 3 – Right to Free Elections

Signatory States undertake to hold free elections at reasonable intervals by secret ballot under conditions which will ensure the free expression of the opinion of the people in the choice of the legislature.

Articles 1 & 2 Sixth Protocol

Article 1 – Abolition of Death Penalty

The death penalty shall be abolished. No one shall be condemned to such penalty or executed.

Article 2 – Death Penalty in time of War

A State may make provision in its law for the death penalty in respect of acts committed in time of war or of its imminent threat (such a penalty must be applied in accordance with a national law and the State must communicate the relevant provision to the Secretary General of the Council of Europe).

All the above rights and freedoms must be read with Articles 16 – 18 of the Convention which are as follows.

Articles 16–18 Convention Rights & Freedoms

Article 16 – Restrictions on Political Activity of Aliens

Nothing in Articles 10, 11 &14 shall be regarded as preventing the signatories from imposing restrictions on the political activity of aliens.

Article 17 – Prohibition of Abuse of Rights

Nothing in this Convention may be interpreted as implying for any State, group or person any right to engage in any activity or perform any act aimed at the destruction of any of the rights and freedoms set forth herein, or at their limitation to a greater extent than is provided for in the Convention.

Article 18 – Limitation on Use of Restriction of Rights

Restrictions permitted under this Convention to the said rights and freedoms shall not be applied for any purpose other than those for which they have been prescribed.

Designated Derogation and Reservation

Convention Articles summarised in preceding pages are to have effect for the purposes of HRA 1998, subject to any:

- **'Designated Derogation'** [time limited capacity for the Secretary of State to suspend

either Article 5(3) (arrest and detention under
right to liberty and security) or any other
specified Article or Protocol] [s.14 HRA 1998], or

- **'Designated Reservation'** [i.e. the UK's
  reservation about the Education provision
  implied by Protocol 1 Article 2, second sentence
  which is elaborated upon in Part 11 of Sch.3]
  [s.15 HRA 1998] or

- **Other reservation** set out in an order made by
  the Secretary of State.

*NB. The Secretary of State may be order make such
amendments to this Act as s/he considers
appropriate to reflect the effect, in relation to the UK
of a Protocol to the convention which the UK has
ratified or has signed with a view to ratification
[s.1(4) &(5)]. No amendment may be made by such
an order so as to come into force before the Protocol
concerned is in force in the UK [s.1 (6)].*

Appendix 2: Human Rights Act 1998

Interpretation of Convention Rights [s.2 HRA 1998]

■ A court or tribunal determining a question which has arisen in connection with a Convention right must take into account in accordance with rules, any relevant judgement, decision, declaration or advisory opinion of the European Court of Human Rights, opinion or decision formally provided by the Commission or any decision made by the Committee of Ministers.

Interpretation of Legislation [s.3 HRA 1998]

■ So far as it is possible to do so, primary and subordinate legislation must be read and given effect in a way which is compatible with Convention rights.

■ The above provision applies:

- Whenever the primary and subordinate legislation was enacted and
- Does not affect validity, continuing operation or enforcement of any incompatible primary legislation and
- Does not affect the validity, continuing operation or enforcement of any incompatible subordinate legislation if (disregarding any

possibility of revocation) primary legislation
prevents removal of the incompatibility.

Declaration of Incompatibility [s.4 HRA 1998]

■ If a court determines that the provision of primary or
subordinate legislation is incompatible with a
Convention right, it may make a declaration of that
incompatibility [s.4 (1) – (3) HRA 1998].

*Court in this section means House of Lords, Judicial
Committee of the Privy Council, Courts Martial Appeal
Court and in England and the High Court or the Court of
Appeal [s.4(5) HRA 1998]*

■ A declaration of incompatibility:
  • Does not affect the validity, continuing
    operation or enforcement of the provision in
    respect of which it is given and
  • Is not binding on the parties to the proceedings
    in which it is made [s.4(6) HRA 1998]

*Where a court is considering whether to make a
declaration of incompatibility, the Crown is entitled to
notice in accordance with rules of court and may be
joined as a party to the proceedings [s.5 HRA 1998].*

Act of Public Authorities [s.6 (1) HRA 1998]

■ It is unlawful for a 'public authority' to act in a way
which is incompatible with a Convention right

*A public authority includes a court or tribunal and any
person certain of whose functions are functions of a*

public nature, but does not include either House of Parliament or a person exercising functions in connection with proceedings in Parliament.

- ■ A person who claims that a public authority has acted (or proposes to act) in a way which is made unlawful by s.6(1) may:

  - • Bring proceedings against the authority under this Act in the appropriate court or tribunal or
  - • Rely on the Convention right/s concerned in any legal proceedings,
  - • But only if s/he is (or would be) a victim of the unlawful act [s.7 (1)].

  NB. Time limits do or may, in accordance with rules of court be applied to bringing such proceedings [s.1(5)] which may only be brought exercising a right of appeal on an application for judicial review or in such courts may be prescribed in rules [s.9(1)].

Power to Take Remedial Action [s.10 HRA 1998]

- ■ If a provision of legislation has been declared to be incompatible with a Convention right and:

  - • All those eligible to appeal confirm in writing that they do not intend to do so, the time limit has expired or an appeal initiated has been determined or
  - • The Crown determines that to achieve compatibility with European Convention obligations, primary or secondary legislation needs amending

- A Minister of the Crown may by order make such amendments as s/he considers necessary

Freedom of Thought, Conscience & Religion [s.13 HRA 1998]

■ If a court (including a tribunal) determines that any question arising under this Act might affect the exercise by a religious organisation (itself or its members collectively) of the Convention right to freedom of thought, conscience and religion it must have particular regard to the importance of that right.

Parliamentary Statement of Compatibility [s.19 HRA 1998]

■ A Minister of the Crown in charge of a Bill must before its second reading :

- Make a written statement to the effect that the Bill's provisions are compatible with the Convention's rights or
- Make a written statement to the effect that although s/he is unable to make a statement of compatibility, the government nevertheless wishes to proceed with the Bill.

Appendix 3: CAE Publications

■ This guide to the Children (Scotland) Act 1995 is CAE's first publication covering legislation relevant to Scotland.

■ Further copies may be ordered from: 105 Bishops Park, Mid Calder, West Lothian EH53 0SR. email: childactScotland@dsl.pipex.com

■ The following 'Personal Guides' relevant to England and/or Wales are available from CAE's English office at: 103 Mayfield Road South Croydon Surrey CR2 0BH tel: 020 8651 0554 fax: 020 8405 8483 email: childact@dial.pipex.com

- Children Act 1989 in the Context of the Human Rights Act 1998
- Children Act 2004
- Child Protection
- Residential Care of Children
- Fostering
- 'How Old Do I Have To Be...?' (simple guide to the rights and responsibilities of 0–21 year olds)
- Domestic Violence – (Part IV Family Law Act 1996 & Protection from Harassment Act 1997)
- Crime and Disorder Act 1998
- Sexual Offences Act 2003
- Anti Social Behaviour
- Childcare Act 2006

www.caeuk.org

Discounts for orders of 50 or more of any one title